ITALIAN PICTURES OF THE RENAISSANCE

A LIST OF THE PRINCIPAL ARTISTS
AND THEIR WORKS
WITH AN INDEX OF PLACES

BY

BERNARD BERENSON

FLORENTINE SCHOOL
IN TWO VOLUMES

VOL. II

WITH 888 ILLUSTRATIONS

PHAIDON PUBLISHERS INC
DISTRIBUTED BY
NEW YORK GRAPHIC SOCIETY PUBLISHERS LTD
GREENWICH · CONNECTICUT

19174

PHAIDON PRESS LTD · LONDON SW7

PRINTED IN GREAT BRITAIN

FLORENTINE PICTURES
OF THE RENAISSANCE

PLATES

591—1478

591. ANGELICO: *Music-making Angel. Detail of Plate 600.*

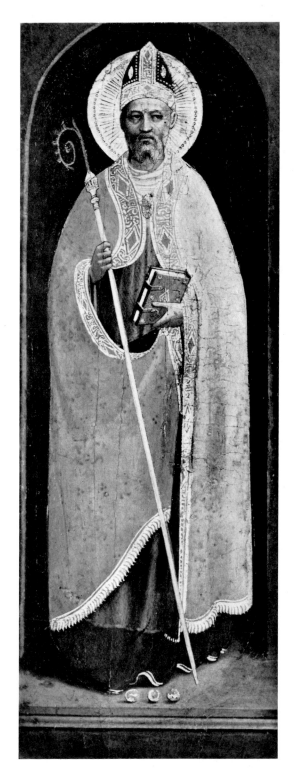 

592–93. ANGELICO: *S. Nicholas and S. Michael (two panels from the frame of the S. Domenico di Fiesole altarpiece).* Formerly Sheffield, Rev. A. Hawkins-Jones.

594. ANGELICO: *Madonna and Child with Angels and Saints (detail)*. Florence, S. Domenico di Fiesole.

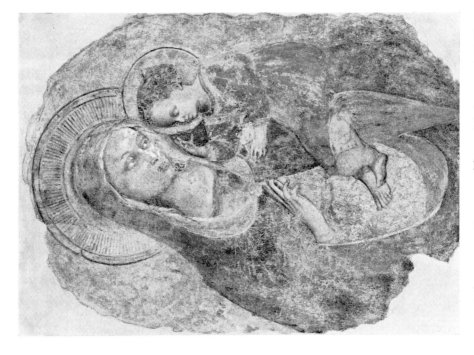

596. ANGELICO: *Fragment of fresco: Madonna and Child.*
Florence, S. Domenico di Fiesole.

595. ANGELICO: *Fresco from S. Domenico di Fiesole: Madonna and Child with SS. Dominic
and Thomas Aquinas. Leningrad, Hermitage.*

597. Angelico: *The Elect* (*detail of Last Judgement*). Florence, Museo di S. Marco.

598. ANGELICO: *Madonna and Child with four Angels.*
Detroit, Institute of Art.

599. ANGELICO: *S. Peter preaching (from the predella of the Tabernacolo dei Linaiuoli).* Florence,
Museo di S. Marco. *1433.*

600. ANGELICO: *Tabernacolo dei Linaiuoli* (open). Florence, Museo di S. Marco. *1433.*

601. ANGELICO: *The S. Domenico Triptych: Madonna and Child with four Angels; SS. John Evangelist, John Baptist, Mark and Mary Magdalen; in pinnacles, Crucifixion, Annunciation.* Cortona, Museo Diocesano.

603. ANGELICO: *Raising of Napoleone Orsini (detail of predella to S. Domenico Triptych).* Cortona, Museo Diocesano.

602. ANGELICO: *Expulsion from Paradise (detail of Plate 604).*

604. ANGELICO: *Annunciation;* in predella, *Life of the Virgin and two Stories of S. Dominic.*
Cortona, Museo Diocesano.

605. ANGELICO: *Visitation (detail from plate 604).* Cortona, Museo Diocesano.

606. ANGELICO: *Madonna and Child with four Angels (central panel of triptych).* Perugia, Pinacoteca. *1437.*

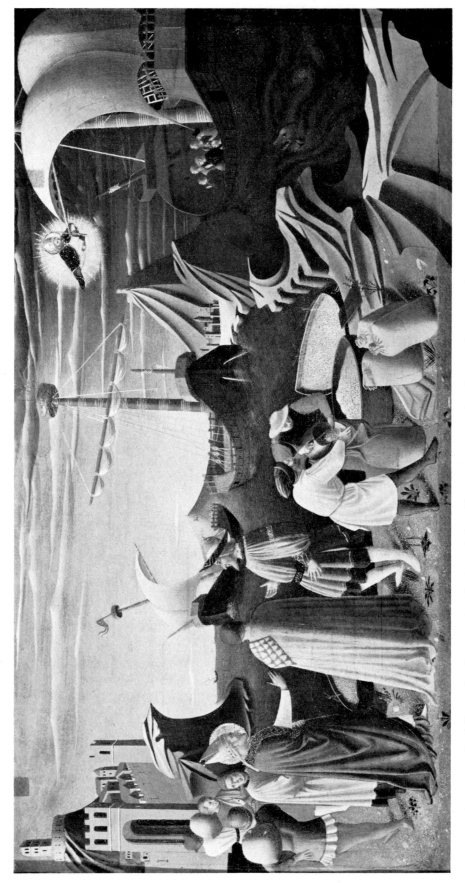

607. ANGELICO: *Predella panel to Perugia triptych: S. Nicholas addressing an Imperial Embassy and saving a Ship at Sea. Rome, Pinacoteca Vaticana. 1437.*

608. ANGELICO: *Deposition*; in pilasters of frame, *sixteen Saints* (pinnacles by Lorenzo Monaco). Florence, Museo di S. Marco.

609. ANGELICO: *Head of S. Lawrence from the S. Marco Altarpiece*. Florence, Museo di S. Marco. *1438/40*.

610. ANGELICO: *S. Marco Altarpiece: Madonna and Child with Angels and SS. Lawrence, John Evangelist, Mark, Cosmas, Damian, Dominic, Francis and Peter Martyr.* Florence, Museo di S. Marco. *1438/40.*

611. ANGELICO: *Annalena Altarpiece: Madonna and Child with SS. Peter Martyr, Cosmas, Damian, John Evangelist, Lawrence and Francis.* Florence, Museo di S. Marco.

612–13. ANGELICO and Assistants: *Two panels from the dismembered predella of the Annalena Altarpiece:*
Dream of the Deacon Justinian—Northwick Park, Capt. Spencer-Churchill;
SS. Cosmas and Damian before Lycias—Florence, Museo di S. Marco.

614–15. ANGELICO: *Two panels from the dismembered predella of the S. Marco Altarpiece: Beheading of SS. Cosmas and Damian*—Paris, Louvre; *Burial of SS. Cosmas and Damian*—Florence, Museo di S. Marco. *1438/40.*

616. ANGELICO: *Fresco: Annunciation*. Florence, Convento di S. Marco, Third Cell. *1439/45*.

617. ANGELICO: *Fresco: Transfiguration*. Florence, Convento di S. Marco, Sixth Cell. *1439/45*.

618. ANGELICO: *Fresco: The meditating S. Dominic in the Mocking of Christ*. Florence, Convento di S. Marco, Seventh Cell. *1439/45*.

619. ANGELICO: *Fresco: Madonna and Child with Saints (detail)*. Florence, Convento di S. Marco, Upper Corridor.

620. ANGELICO and Assistants: *Madonna of Humility*. Turin, Pinacoteca.

621. ANGELICO: *Bosco ai Frati Altarpiece: Madonna and Child with Angels and SS. Anthony of Padua, Louis of Toulouse, Francis, Cosmas, Damian and Peter Martyr*. Florence, Museo di S. Marco.

622. ANGELICO, assisted by GOZZOLI: Frescoes: *Christ in Judgement, Angels and Prophets.* Orvieto, Duomo, Cappella di S. Brizio. 1447.

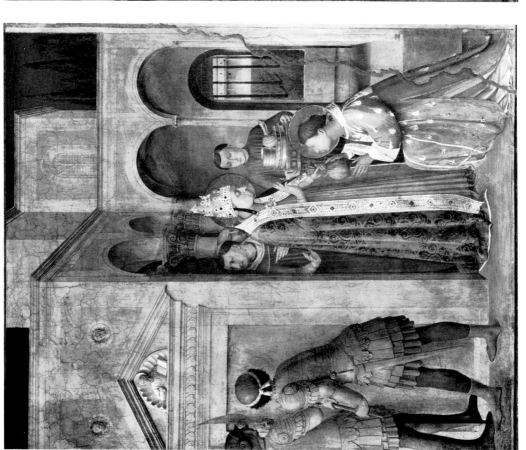

623–24. ANGELICO: *Frescoes: S. Lawrence receiving the Treasures of the Church from Pope Sixtus II; Stoning of S. Stephen. Rome, Vatican, Cappella Niccolina. 1447/49.*

625. ANGELICO: *Crucifixion with Cardinal Giovanni Torquemada as Donor.*
Cambridge (Mass.), Fogg Art Museum.

626. ANGELICO and Assistants: Door of the Silver Chest of the SS. Annunziata: *Annunciation, Nativity, Circumcision, Massacre of Innocents, Flight into Egypt (the Allegorical Wheel, by Domenico di Michelino).* Florence, Museo di S. Marco. *From 1448.*

628. ZANOBI STROZZI: *Marriage of S. Catherine*, in the Antiphonary from S. Gaggio. Florence, Principe Corsini. *1447.*

627. ZANOBI STROZZI: *Illuminated Initial: Penitent Youth blessed by God the Father.* Florence, Museo di S. Marco, Antiphonary D. *1446.*

630. DOMENICO DI MICHELINO: *Madonna of Humility with two music-making Angels*. Milan, Mario Crespi.

629. DOMENICO DI MICHELINO (?): *Madonna and Child with four Angels*. Florence, Museo di S. Marco.

631. Domenico di Michelino: *Annunciation.*
Philadelphia, Johnson Collection.

632. Domenico di Michelino: *Madonna and Child with Angels and SS. Cosmas, Damian, Jerome, John Baptist, Francis and Lawrence; six Saints in pilasters; Man of Sorrows and Life of S. Jerome in predella.* Chartres, Musée.

633. DOMENICO DI MICHELINO: *John Paleologus setting out for Venice.*
Williamstown (Mass.), Clark Art Institute.

634. DOMENICO DI MICHELINO: *Journey of the Magi.* Strasbourg, Musée.

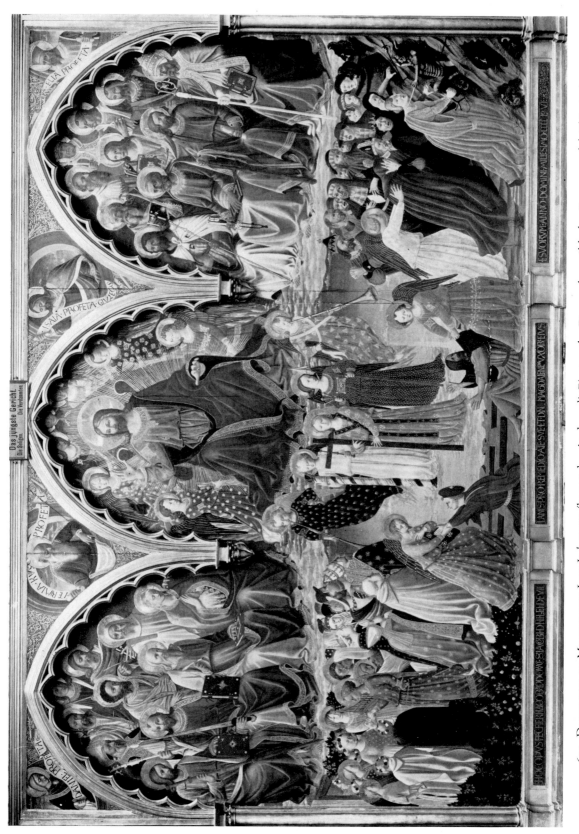

635. DOMENICO DI MICHELINO: *Last Judgement* (begun by Andrea di Giusto; the Damned possibly by Francesco del Chierico).
Berlin, Staatliche Museen. (Destroyed 1945). *Dated 1456.*

637. DOMENICO DI MICHELINO: *Madonna and Child with four Saints.*
Formerly Providence, Rhode Island School of Design.

636. DOMENICO DI MICHELINO: *Assumption with SS. Jerome and Francis.*
Dublin, National Gallery of Ireland.

QVI COELVM CECINIT MEDIVM QVE IMVM QVE TRIBVNAL🙟 LVSTRAVIT QVE ANIMO CVNCTA POETA SVO🙟 DOCTVS ADEST DANTES SVA QVEM FLORENTIA SAEPI🙟
SENSIT CONSILIIS AC PIETATE PATREM🙟 NIL POTVIT TANTO MORS SAEVA NOCERE POETAE🙟 QVEM VIVVM VIRTVS CARMEN IMAGO FACIT🙟

638. DOMENICO DI MICHELINO: *Fresco: Dante explaining to Florence the Divina Comedia.* Florence, Duomo. *1465.*

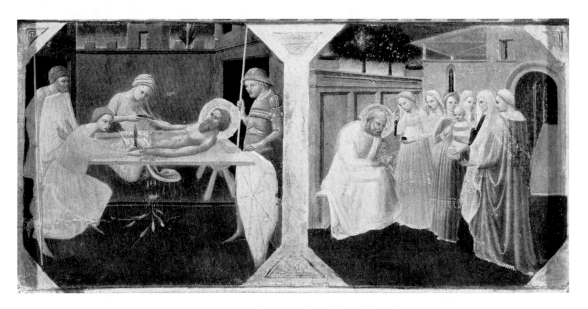

639. ANDREA DI GIUSTO: *Detail from Plate 640.*

640. ANDREA DI GIUSTO: *Triptych of S. Bartolomeo alle Sacca: Madonna and Child, SS. Bartholomew, John Baptist, Benedict, Margaret;* in pinnacles, *Saviour and Annunciation;* in predella, *Flaying of S. Bartholomew, Naming of S. John Baptist, S. Maurus, Nativity, S. Placidus, Death of S. Benedict, Abduction of S. Margaret.* Prato, Pinacoteca. *Dated 1435.*

641. ANDREA DI GIUSTO: *Portable altarpiece: Madonna and Child with Angels; SS. Francis and Clare, SS. Margaret and George; Annunciation.* Turin, Gualino Collection.

642. ANDREA DI GIUSTO: *Adoration of Magi and Saints (detail)*. Figline, S. Andrea a Ripalta. *Dated 1436.*

643. ANDREA DI GIUSTO: *Madonna della Cintola with Saints (detail)*. Florence, Accademia. *Signed and dated 1437.*

644. ANDREA DI GIUSTO: *Portable altarpiece (detail)*. Florence, Accademia.

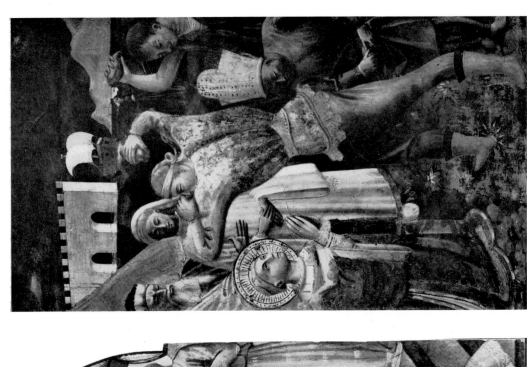

646. ANDREA DI GIUSTO: *Fresco: Stoning of S. Stephen (detail)*. Prato, Duomo.

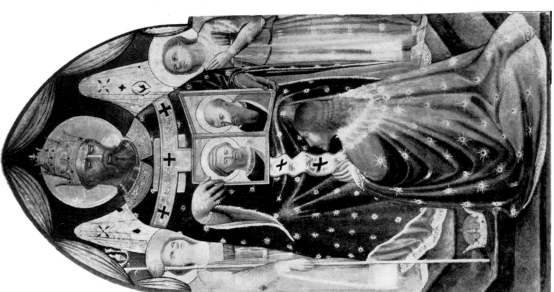

645. ANDREA DI GIUSTO: *Left and centre panels of triptych from the Alberici Collection in Rome: Constantine baptized by Pope Sylvester and Constantine shown the images of SS. Peter and Paul*. Leningrad, Hermitage.

647. ANDREA DI GIUSTO: *Fresco: S. Stephen buried with S. Lawrence.* Prato, Duomo, Cappella dell' Assunta.

648. BARTOLOMEO DI ANDREA BOCCHI: *Triptych: Madonna and Child with Angels; SS. Hippolytus, James,*
Michael and Stephen; in pinnacles, *Christ blessing and Annunciation.* Serravalle Pistoiese, S. Michele.
Signed and dated 1439.

649. BARTOLOMEO DI ANDREA BOCCHI: *Triptych: Madonna della Cintola; SS. James, John Evangelist, Peter and Paul*. Warsaw, Museum. *Signed.*

650. MARIOTTO DI CRISTOFANO: *Resurrection (back of the Ospedale di S. Matteo Altarpiece)*. Florence, Accademia. *1445/47.*

651. MARIOTTO DI CRISTOFANO: *Marriage of S. Catherine with SS. Dorothy, Agnes, Mary Magdalen and Elizabeth of Hungary (front of the Ospedale di S. Matteo Altarpiece)*. Florence, Accademia. *1445/47*.

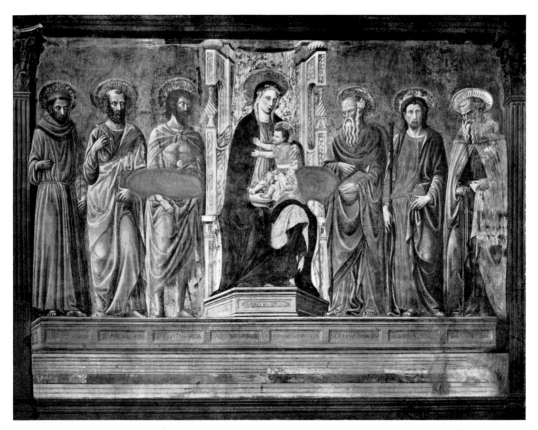

652. PAOLO SCHIAVO: *Fresco: Madonna and Child with SS. Francis, Mark, John Baptist, John Evangelist and Anthony Abbot*. Florence, S. Miniato al Monte. *Signed and dated 1436.*

653. PAOLO SCHIAVO: *Fresco: Crucifixion with adoring Nuns*. Florence, Museo del Castagno (ex-Convent of S. Apollonia). *Signed and dated 1448.*

654. PAOLO SCHIAVO: *Triptych: Annunciation; S. Jerome, S. Lawrence. Berlin and Berlin-Ost, Staatliche Museen.*

656. PAOLO SCHIAVO: *Fresco: Madonna of Humility and two Angels.*
Vespignano, S. Martino.

655. PAOLO SCHIAVO: *Fresco: Madonna and Child with SS. Peter and Paul.*
San Piero a Sieve, Tabernacolo delle Mozzette.

657–58. Florentine close to UCCELLO: *Frescoes: Lamech slaying Cain and Building of the Ark; the family of Adam.*
Florence, S. Maria Novella, Chiostro Verde, East Wall.

659. UCCELLO: *Fresco: Creation of Animals and Creation of Man*. Florence, S. Maria Novella, Chiostro Verde.

660. UCCELLO: *Fresco: Fall of Man (detail)*. Florence, S. Maria Novella, Chiostro Verde.

661. UCCELLO: *Fresco: Equestrian portrait of Sir John Hawkwood*. Florence, Duomo, Left Wall. *1436*.

662. UCCELLO: *Frescoes: Three Heads of Prophets on the Clock-face.* Florence, Duomo, Entrance Wall. *1443.*

663. UCCELLO: *Fresco: Sacrifice of Noah (detail)*. Florence, S. Maria Novella, Chiostro Verde.

664. UCCELLO: *Fresco: The Flood (detail)*. Florence, S. Maria Novella, Chiostro Verde.

665. UCCELLO: *The Rout of S. Romano (detail)*. London, National Gallery.

666. UCCELLO: *S. George killing the Dragon* (*detail*). London, National Gallery.

667, 668. UCCELLO: *The Host restored to the Altar; The Execution of the repentant Woman (details of predella with Story of the Profanation of the Host).* Urbino, Galleria Nazionale delle Marche.

669. UCCELLO: *A Woman redeems her cloak at the price of a consecrated Host (detail of predella)*.
Urbino, Galleria Nazionale delle Marche.

670, 671. Florentine between MASACCIO and UCCELLO: *Two predella panels: S. Quiricus slapping the Judge; Accusation of SS. Quiricus and Julitta.* Highnam Court, Gambier-Parry Collection.

672, 673. GIOVANNI DI FRANCESCO: *Frescoes: Disputation of S. Stephen; Birth of the Virgin.*
Prato, Duomo, Cappella Bocchineri.

674. GIOVANNI DI FRANCESCO: *A Nun and Worshippers.*
Florence, Contini Bonacossi Collection.

675. GIOVANNI DI FRANCESCO: *Nativity, with SS. Jerome, Mary Magdalen and Eustace.*
Karlsruhe, Kunsthalle.

676. GIOVANNI DI FRANCESCO: *Detail of the Karlsruhe Nativity* (plate 675).

677. GIOVANNI DI FRANCESCO: *Predella panel: Crucifixion with SS. Francis and John the Baptist.*
Lugano, Thyssen Collection.

678. GIOVANNI DI FRANCESCO: *Detail of the Karlsruhe Nativity* (plate 675).

679. GIOVANNI DI FRANCESCO: *Episodes of Monastic Life (detail)*. Florence, Accademia.

680. Florentine close to GIOVANNI DI FRANCESCO: *Smaller Thebaid (detail)*. Balcarres, Earl of Crawford and Balcarres.

681. Florentine between GIOVANNI DI FRANCESCO and NERI DI BICCI: *Large Thebaid (detail)*. Balcarres, Earl of Crawford and Balcarres.

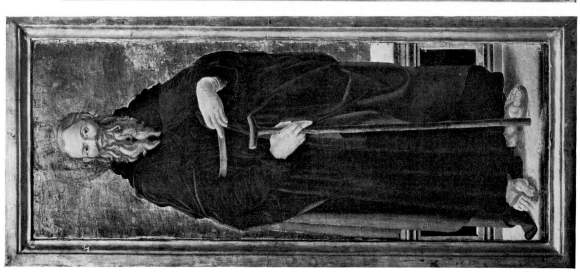

682. GIOVANNI DI FRANCESCO: *Fragments of Triptych: Madonna and Child*—Florence, Contini Bonacossi Collection; *S. Anthony Abbot*, Milan, Brizio Collection; *S. James*, Lyons, Musée

684. GIOVANNI DI FRANCESCO: *Fresco: Apostle (detail).* Morrocco, S. Maria.

683. GIOVANNI DI FRANCESCO: *Altar frontal: S. Blaise (detail).* Florence, S. Biagio a Petriolo. *Dated 1453.*

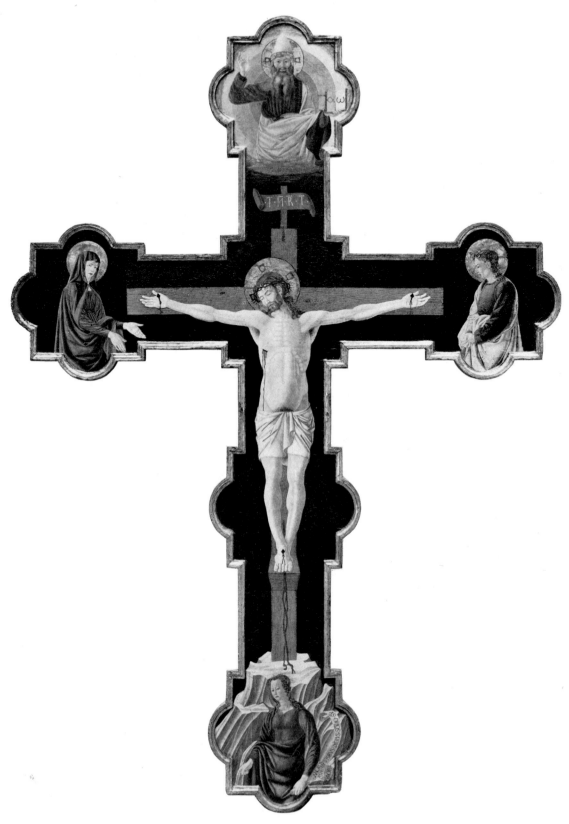

685. GIOVANNI DI FRANCESCO: *Painted Cross from S. Andrea a Brozzi.*
Florence, Seminario Maggiore.

686. GIOVANNI DI FRANCESCO: *Frescoed Lunette: God the Father and the martyred Innocents.*
Florence, Spedale degli Innocenti, Portico.

687. GIOVANNI DI FRANCESCO: *Annunciation (pinnacle of Carrand Triptych)*. Florence, Bargello.

688. GIOVANNI DI FRANCESCO: *The Carrand Triptych: Madonna and Child; SS. Francis, John Baptist, Nicholas and Peter;
in pinnacles, Annunciation, Coronation, Madonna della Cintola. Florence, Bargello.*

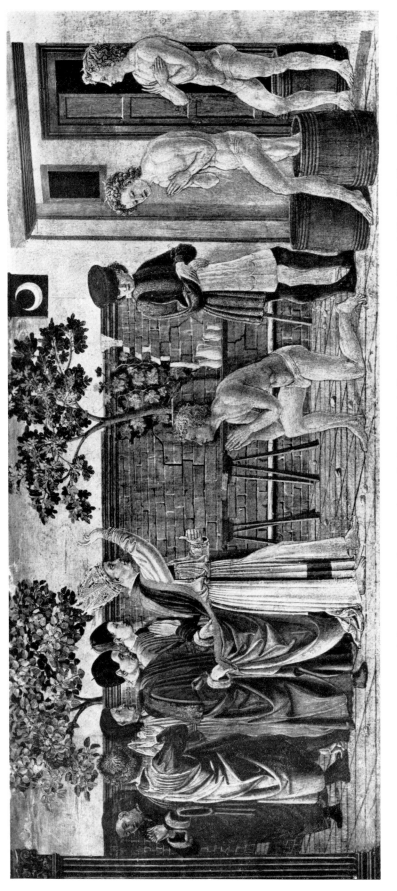

689. Giovanni di Francesco: S. Nicholas raising the three Youths in the barrels (probably predella panel of Carrand Triptych). Florence, Casa Buonarroti.

690. GIOVANNI DI FRANCESCO: *Coronation (pinnacle of Carrand Triptych)*. Florence, Bargello.

691. GIOVANNI DI FRANCESCO (?): *Triptych: Madonna and Child with two Angels, SS. Bridget and Michael*.
New York, Hugh Satterlee.

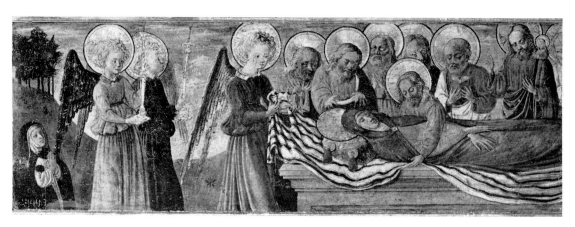

692–94. GIOVANNI DI FRANCESCO (?): *Parts of the altarpiece from S. Giovanni Evangelista at Pratovecchio:
SS. Michael and John the Baptist*—London, National Gallery; *Virgin in Glory with Cherubim*—Florence,
Gallerie Fiorentine; *Dormition of the Virgin with female donor (detail)*—Boston, Gardner Museum.

695. MASTER OF THE BARBERINI PANELS: *Annunciation*. Washington, National Gallery of Art, Kress Collection. *ca 1450*.

696. MASTER OF THE BARBERINI PANELS: *Detail of Presentation* (*plate 697*). Boston, Museum of Fine Arts.

697. MASTER OF THE BARBERINI PANELS: *Barberini Panel: Presentation of the Virgin.*
Boston, Museum of Fine Arts. *ca 1465/70.*

698. MASTER OF THE BARBERINI PANELS: *Barberini Panel: Birth of the Virgin*. New York,
Metropolitan Museum. *ca 1465/70*.

699. MASTER OF THE BARBERINI PANELS: *Detail from Birth of the Virgin (plate 698).* New York, Metropolitan Museum.

700. DOMENICO VENEZIANO and Assistants: *Desco: Solomon and the Queen of Sheba (detail)*.
Houston (Texas), Museum of Fine Arts.

701. DOMENICO VENEZIANO: *Tondo: Adoration of Magi*. Berlin, Staatliche Museen.

702. DOMENICO VENEZIANO: *Profile portrait of Lady*.
Boston, Gardner Museum.

703. DOMENICO VENEZIANO: *Profile portrait of Lady*.
London, National Gallery.

704. DOMENICO VENEZIANO: *Matteo Olivieri*.
Washington, National Gallery of Art,
Mellon Collection.

705. DOMENICO VENEZIANO: *Michele Olivieri*.
New York, Mrs. J. D. Rockefeller, Jr.

706. DOMENICO VENEZIANO: *Fresco from the Tabernacolo del Canto de' Carnesecchi:*
Madonna and Child. London, National Gallery. *Signed. ca 1439.*

707. Domenico Veneziano: *Madonna and Child against hedge of roses*. Bucharest, Museum.

708. DOMENICO VENEZIANO: *Madonna and Child against hedge of roses*. Washington, National Gallery of Art, Kress Collection.

709–10. Domenico Veneziano: *Two predella panels of the S. Lucia dei Magnoli altarpiece:*
Miracle of S. Zenobius—Cambridge, Fitzwilliam Museum; *Martyrdom of S. Lucy*—
Berlin, Staatliche Museen.

712. FRANCESCO DI ANTONIO: *Madonna and Child with ten Angels.*
Cologne, Wallraf-Richartz Museum.

711. FRANCESCO DI ANTONIO: *Fresco: Annunciation with donor.*
Figline, S. Francesco.

713. FRANCESCO DI ANTONIO: *Triptych: Madonna and Child, SS. Laurence, and John Gualbert, (detail) in pinnacles.* Cambridge, Fitzwilliam Museum. *Signed and dated 1415.*

714–717. FRANCESCO DI ANTONIO: *Madonna and Child with six Angels, SS. John Baptist and Jerome;* above, *God the Father, Annunciation, two Prophets*—Grenoble, Musée; *Predella panels to Grenoble Triptych: Vision of S. Benedict and S. Benedict announcing his Death to his Brethren; Dream of S. Jerome; Death of S. Benedict.* Paris, Musées Nationaux.

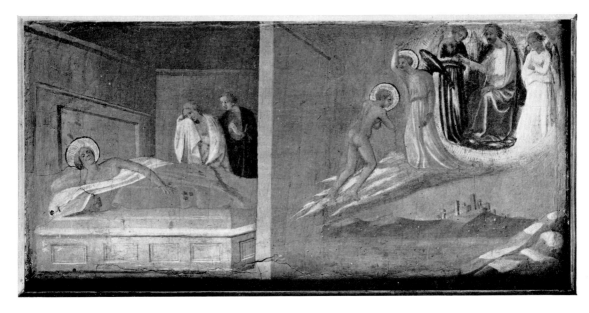

718. FRANCESCO DI ANTONIO: *Organshutter from Orsanmichele in Florence (outside):
The Evangelists Mark and Luke*. Formerly Florence, Accademia. *1429.*

719. FRANCESCO DI ANTONIO: *Organshutter from Orsanmichele in Florence (inside):*
Four singing Angels. Formerly Florence, Accademia. *1429.*

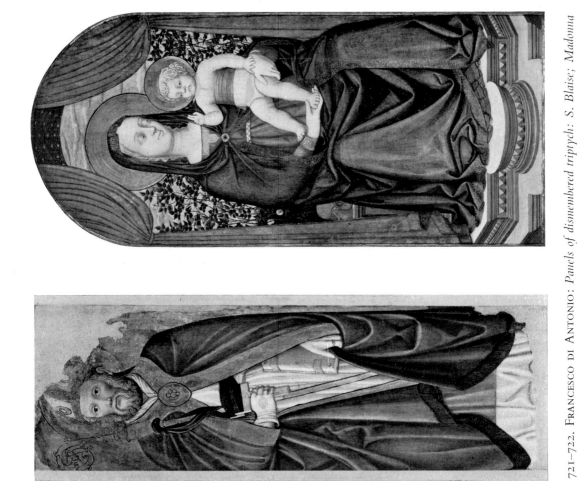

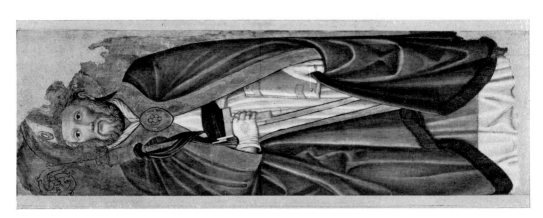

721–722. Francesco di Antonio: *Panels of dismembered triptych: S. Blaise; Madonna and Child.* San Giovanni Valdarno, Museo.

720. Francesco di Antonio: *Madonna and Child eating grapes.* Homeless.

723. Francesco di Antonio: *Madonna and Child appearing to S. Sebastian and to SS. Lazarus, Mary Magdalen and Martha on the voyage to Marseilles.* Fucecchio, Museo.

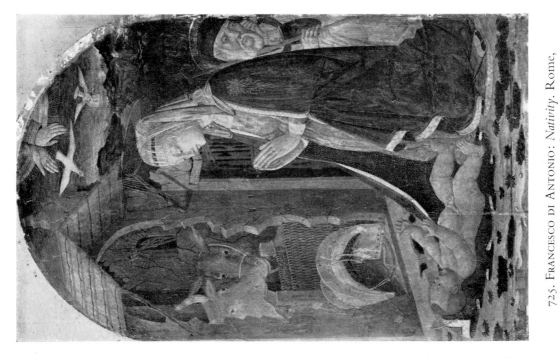

725. Francesco di Antonio: *Nativity*. Rome,
Comm. Arduino Colasanti.

724. Francesco di Antonio: *Frescoed Tabernacle: Madonna
and Child, two Angels, S. John Baptist and a Bishop Saint.*
Florence, Piazza S. Maria Novella.

727. Francesco di Antonio: *Madonna and Child.* Homeless.

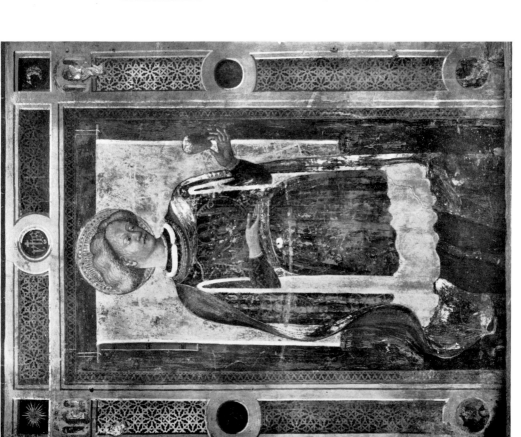

726. Francesco di Antonio: *Fresco: S. Ansanus.* Florence,
S. Niccolò Oltrarno.

728. FRANCESCO DI ANTONIO: *Cassone: Feud of two Florentine Families*. Copenhagen, Statensmuseum.

729. FRANCESCO DI ANTONIO: *Cassone panel: Triumph of Fame*. Formerly Milan, Chiesa Collection.

730. Francesco di Antonio: *Detail of the Feud, with view of Florence*. Copenhagen, Statensmuseum.

731. Francesco di Antonio: *Tondo: 'Il Giuoco del Civettino'*. Florence, Palazzo Davanzati.

733a. Francesco di Antonio: *The Adimari Cassone (left half)*. Florence, Accademia.

732. FRANCESCO DI ANTONIO on design by DOMENICO VENEZIANO: *Desco da Parto for Lorenzo de' Medici: Triumph of Fame*. New York, Historical Society. *1449*.

733b. FRANCESCO DI ANTONIO: *The Adimari Cassone (right half)*. Florence, Accademia.

734. APOLLONIO DI GIOVANNI: *Cassone: A Tournament*. London, National Gallery.

736a. APOLLONIO DI GIOVANNI: *Cassone panel: Scenes from the Odyssey (left half)*. Chicago, Art Institute

735. APOLLONIO DI GIOVANNI: *Detail of Plate 734.*

5b. APOLLONIO DI GIOVANNI: *Cassone panel: Scenes from the Odyssey (right half).* Chicago, Art Institute.

737–739. APOLLONIO DI GIOVANNI: *Three details from the Jarves Cassoni with Scenes from the Aeneid: Venus asks Aeolus to start a tempest; Venus summons Aeneas and Achates; Work on the Walls of Carthage.* New Haven, Yale University.

740–742. APOLLONIO DI GIOVANNI: *Three miniatures from the Aeneid: Venus starting a storm; Venus summoning Aeneas and Achates; Meeting of Aeneas and Dido while the walls of Carthago are being built.* Florence, Biblioteca Riccardiana, codex 492.

743, 744. APOLLONIO DI GIOVANNI: *Two details of the Jarves Cassone panel with Solomon and the Queen of Sheba.* New Haven, Yale University.

745. APOLLONIO DI GIOVANNI: *Cassone panel with a Tournament*. Oxford, Ashmolean Museum.

746. APOLLONIO DI GIOVANNI: *Cassone panel with Triumph of Aemilius Paullus*. Cambridge, Fitzwilliam Museum.

747. ANTONIO DA FIRENZE: *Front of Gonfalone: Madonna and Child with two Angels,
SS. Liberius and John Baptist.* Leningrad, Hermitage. *Signed.*

748. ANTONIO DA FIRENZE: *Two panels from a dismembered altarpiece: S. Zenobius and the Blessed Filippo Benizzi, S. Martin of Todi and the Blessed Pellegrino da Forlì.* Venice, Accademia. *Signed twice.*

749. ANDREA DEL CASTAGNO: *Fresco from the Castello del Trebbio:*
Detail of Madonna and Child with Angels, SS. John Baptist and Jerome, and two children.
Florence, Contini Bonacossi Collection.

750–751. ANDREA DEL CASTAGNO: *Frescoes: Two details of Prophets and Putti.* Venice, S. Zaccaria,
Cappella di S. Tarasio, Vault. *Signed and dated 1442.*

752. ANDREA DEL CASTAGNO: *Fresco: S. Zacharias* (*detail.*) Venice, S. Zaccaria, Cappella di S. Tarasio, Vault. *1442.*

753. ANDREA DEL CASTAGNO: *Frescoes: Last Supper, Crucifixion, Entombment, Resurrection.* Florence, former Refectory of the Convent of S. Apollonia, now Museo del Castagno. *1445/50.*

754, 755. ANDREA DEL CASTAGNO: *Frescoes: two details of the Last Supper.* Florence, former Refectory of the
Convent of S. Apollonia, now Museo del Castagno. *1445/50.*

756. ANDREA DEL CASTAGNO: *Fresco: detail of Resurrection*. Florence, former Refectory of the Convent of
S. Apollonia, now Museo del Castagno. *1445/50*.

757. ANDREA DEL CASTAGNO: *Detail of Assumption with SS. Julian and Miniato*. Berlin, Staatliche Museen.
1449/50.

758. ANDREA DEL CASTAGNO: *Assumption with SS. Julian and Miniato.*
Berlin, Staatliche Museen. *1449/50.*

759. ANDREA DEL CASTAGNO: *Fresco from overdoor in the Villa Carducci Pandolfini at Legnaia: Esther.*
Florence, Museo del Castagno.

760. ANDREA DEL CASTAGNO: *Frescoed wall: Madonna and Child under a baldacchino supported by two Angels, Eve.*
Florence, Villa Carducci Pandolfini a Legnaia (Soffiano).

761. ANDREA DEL CASTAGNO: *Fresco: Equestrian portrait of Niccolò da Tolentino.*
Florence, Duomo. *1456.*

762. ANDREA DEL CASTAGNO: *Fresco lunette from the Convento degli Angioli: Christ on the Cross with the Virgin, S. John, S. Benedict and S. Romuald.* Florence, Museo del Castagno.

763. Florentine between CASTAGNO and BOTTICINI: *Christ on the Cross with SS. Jerome and Anthony Abbot.* Argiano, S. Maria e Angelo.

764. ANDREA DEL CASTAGNO: *Detail of fresco lunette from the Convento degli Angioli: the mourning Virgin.*
Florence, Museo del Castagno.

766. Antonio Pollajuolo: *Apollo and Daphne.*
London, National Gallery.

765. Antonio Pollajuolo: *Hercules slaying the Hydra.*
Formerly Florence, Uffizi, ca 1460.

767. Antonio Pollajuolo: *The Rape of Dejaneira.* New Haven, Yale University Gallery. *Before 1467.*

768. Piero Pollajuolo on early design by Antonio: *Communion of S. Mary Magdalen* (from Staggia). Colle Val d'Elsa, Palazzo Vescovile.

769. Details of Plate 773.

770. ANTONIO POLLAJUOLO: *Fresco: Dancing nudes.* Florence, Torre del Gallo. *1465–75.*

771. ANTONIO POLLAJUOLO: *Fresco: Angel drawing aside a curtain*. Florence, S. Miniato al Monte, Cappella dei Portoghesi. *1467*.

772. ANTONIO and PIERO POLLAJUOLO: *SS. Eustace, James and Vincent*
(*from the Cappella dei Portoghesi*). Florence, Uffizi. *1467*.

773. PIERO POLLAJUOLO: *Annunciation*. Berlin, Staatliche Museen.

774. PIERO POLLAJUOLO: *Profile portrait of Woman.*
West Orange (N.J.), Nils B. Herzloff.

775. PIERO POLLAJUOLO: *Profile portrait of Woman.*
Milan, Museo Poldi Pezzoli.

776. ANTONIO POLLAJUOLO: *Gian Galeazzo Sforza.*
Florence, Uffizi.

777. ANTONIO POLLAJUOLO: *Profile portrait of Woman.*
Boston, Gardner Museum.

778. ANTONIO and PIERO POLLAJUOLO: *Tobias and the Angel*. Turin, Pinacoteca.

779. PIERO POLLAJUOLO: *Madonna (destroyed)*. Strasbourg, Museum.

780. PIERO POLLAJUOLO: *Prudence*. Florence, Uffizi. *1470*.

781. *Embroidery, probably on a design by* PIERO POLLAJUOLO: *Sixtus IV kneeling before S. Francis*. Assisi, S. Francesco, Treasury.

782. POLLAJUOLO: *Fragment of fresco: S. Jerome*. Pistoia, S. Domenico.

783, 784. *Two Embroideries on a design by* ANTONIO POLLAJUOLO: *Beheading of Baptist; Salome's Dance.*
Florence, Opera del Duomo, *1466–80.*

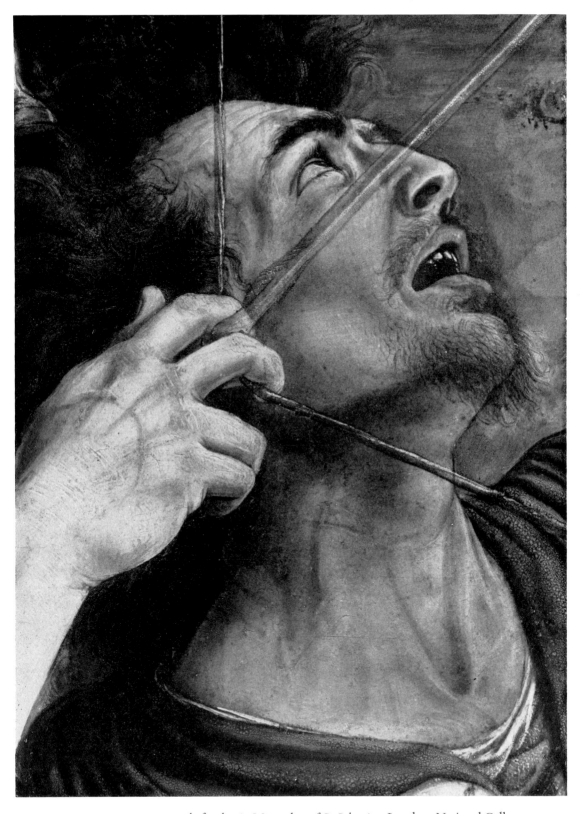

785. ANTONIO POLLAJUOLO: *Detail of archer in Martyrdom of S. Sebastian*. London, National Gallery. *ca 1475*.

786. ANTONIO POLLAJUOLO: *Two details of Martyrdom of S. Sebastian*. London, National Gallery. *ca 1475*.

787. PIERO POLLAJUOLO: *Coronation of the Virgin and Saints*. San Gimignano, S. Agostino. *Signed and dated 1483.*

788. ANTONIO POLLAIUOLO: *Detail of the bronze Monument of Pope Sixtus IV. Rome, S. Pietro. 1493.*

789–790. Crude Imitator of POLLAJUOLO: *Two details of fresco frieze with Labours of Hercules.* Rome, Palazzo Venezia.

791. BALDOVINETTI: *Marriage at Cana, Baptism of Christ (detail of door from silverchest in the SS. Annunziata)*. Florence, Museo di S. Marco. *From 1448 onwards.*

792. BALDOVINETTI: *Profile portrait of Lady*. London, National Gallery.

793. BALDOVINETTI: *Fresco: Nativity (detail of landscape)*. Florence, SS. Annunziata, Atrium. *1460/62.*

794. BALDOVINETTI: *Nativity (intarsia)*. Florence, Duomo, Sacristy. *1463/64.*

795. BALDOVINETTI: *Annunciation*. Florence, Uffizi.

796. BALDOVINETTI: *Fresco in spandrels of Vault: A Prophet.* Florence, S. Miniato al Monte,
Cappella dei Portoghesi. *1466.*

797–799. BALDOVINETTI: *Frescoes in lunettes: Annunciation; Two Evangelists.* Florence, S. Miniato al Monte, Cappella dei Portoghesi. *1466.*

800. BALDOVINETTI: *Fresco: Annunciation (detail)*. Florence, S. Miniato al Monte, Cappella dei Portoghesi. *1466*.

801. BALDOVINETTI: *Fresco: Risen Christ with two Angels (detail)*. Florence, S. Pancrazio, Cappella Rucellai. *1467*.

802. BALDOVINETTI: *Madonna and Saints* (detail). Florence, Uffizi.

803. BALDOVINETTI: *Fresco: Abraham*. Florence, S. Trinita,
Vault of Choir. *1471*.

804. BALDOVINETTI: *Trinity with SS. Benedict and John Gualbert*. Florence, Accademia. *1471*.

805–807. ZANOBI MACHIAVELLI: *Three predella panels: S. Jerome healing the Lion;*
Death of S. Jerome; S. Jerome appearing to S. Augustine. Homeless.

808. ZANOBI MACHIAVELLI: *Madonna and Child with SS. Bernardino, Mark, Louis of Toulouse and Jerome*. Dublin, National Gallery of Ireland. *Signed*.

809. ZANOBI MACHIAVELLI: *Madonna and Child with SS. Anthony of Padua, Silvester, John Baptist and Francis*. Pisa, Museo. *Signed*.

810. ZANOBI MACHIAVELLI: *Madonna and Child with two Angels*. Rome, Palazzo Rospigliosi,
Pallavicini Collection.

811. ZANOBI MACHIAVELLI: *Madonna and Child with SS. Sebastian, Andrew, Bernardino, Paul, Lawrence and Augustine*. Boston, Museum of Fine Arts.

812. ZANOBI MACHIAVELLI: *Predella panel: S. Nicholas of Tolentino saving a Man from Hanging*. Amsterdam, Rijksmuseum.

814. Zanobi Machiavelli: *Annunciation (after Angelico)*. Florence, S. Martino a Mensola.

813. Zanobi Machiavelli: *Left wing of altarpiece:*

816. Zanobi Machiavelli: *Coronation of the Virgin and Saints*. Dijon, Musée. *Signed and dated 1473.*

815. Zanobi Machiavelli: *Right wing of altarpiece:*
S. James. Berlin, Staatliche Museen.
Signed and dated 1463.

818. Florentine between Angelico and Domenico Veneziano: *Madonna and Child.* New York, Metropolitan Museum.

817. Zanobi Machiavelli: *Madonna and Child with Saints and Angels.* Chantilly, Musée.

819. Florentine between ANGELICO and DOMENICO VENEZIANO: 'Lanckoronski' Annunciation. San Francisco, De Young Memorial Museum.

820. PESELLINO: *Madonna and Child with S. Jerome and S. John Baptist*. Philadelphia, Johnson Collection.

821. PESELLINO: *Pinnacle: Crucifixion*. Esztergom, Keresztény Museum.

822. PESELLINO: *Diptych: Annunciation*. Highnam Court, Gambier-Parry Collection.

823. PESELLINO: *Madonna and Child with SS. Anthony Abbot, Jerome, Augustine(?), George and two female Saints.*
New York, Metropolitan Museum.

824, 825. PESELLINO: *Two cassone panels: Triumphs of Love, Chastity and Death; Triumphs of Fame, Time and Eternity.* Boston, Gardner Museum.

826. PESELLINO: *Cassone panel: Story of Griselda.* Bergamo, Accademia Carrara.

827. Pesellino: *Cassone panel: David's early Life (detail)*. Lockinge House, Christopher Lloyd.

828. Pesellino: *Cassone panel: Triumph of David (detail)*. Lockinge House, Christopher Lloyd.

829–830. PESELLINO: *Two predella panels of the Medici Altarpiece from the Cappella del Noviziato in S. Croce: Nativity; S. Anthony of Padua and the Miser's Heart.* Florence, Uffizi. *ca 1450.*

831. FRA FILIPPO LIPPI: *Medici Altarpiece from the Cappella del Noviziato in S. Croce: Madonna and Child with SS. Francis, Damian, Cosmas and Anthony of Padua.* Florence, Uffizi. *ca 1450.*

832. PESELLINO: *Two predella panels of the Medici Altarpiece from the Cappella del Noviziato in S. Croce: S. Francis receiving Stigmata; Dream of the Deacon Justinian.* Paris, Louvre. *ca 1450.*

833. PESELLINO: (completed after his death in the studio of FRA FILIPPO LIPPI; predella by LIPPI, FRA DIAMANTE and MASTER OF S. MINIATO): *Trinity with SS. Zeno, Jerome, James the Great and Mamas; in predella, Stories of the Saints above.* London, National Gallery. *1455/60.*

834. PESELLINO: *Madonna and Child.*
Formerly Lyon, E. Aynard.

835. PESELLINO: *Madonna and Child.*
Ezstergom, Keresztény Museum.

836. PSEUDO PIER FRANCESCO FIORENTINO:
Madonna and Child. Florence, Uffizi. *Dated 1459.*

837. PSEUDO PIER FRANCESCO FIORENTINO:
Madonna and Child. Santa Barbara, University
of California, Sedgwick Collection.

838. Predella panel from PESELLINO's Trinity, executed by the MASTER OF S. MINIATO in FRA FILIPPO's studio: *S. Zeno exorcizing the Daughter of the Emperor Gallienus*. London, National Gallery, 1455/60

840–841. Pseudo Pier Francesco Fiorentino (after Filippo Lippi): *Adoration of the Child*—Cleveland, Museum; *Madonna adoring the Child with Infant S. John, S. Catherine and Angels*. Budapest, Museum.

839. Pseudo Pier Francesco Fiorentino (after Pesellino): *Madonna and Child with Angels, Infant S. John (and S. Francis?)*. Homeless.

842. FRA FILIPPO LIPPI: *Fresco: Confirmation of the Carmelite Order (detail)*.
Florence, S. Maria del Carmine, Cloister. *1432*.

843. FRA FILIPPO LIPPI: *Pinnacle: Madonna of Humility with six Angels and three Saints.*
Milan, Castello Sforzesco.

844. FRA FILIPPO LIPPI: *Madonna and Child with Angels,*
S. Michael, S. Bernard and S. Bartholomew.
Empoli, Museo della Collegiata.

845. FRA FILIPPO LIPPI: *Madonna and Child with Angels,*
Saints and Donor. Venice, Conte Vittorio Cini.

846. FRA FILIPPO LIPPI: *Madonna and Child (from Tarquinia)*. Rome, Galleria Nazionale. *Dated 1437*.

847. FRA FILIPPO LIPPI: *Profile portrait of Lady*. Berlin, Staatliche Museen.

848. FRA FILIPPO LIPPI: *The Virgin receiving the news of her approaching death (detail from predella panel to the Barbadori Altarpiece)*. Florence, Uffizi. *1437*.

849. FRA FILIPPO LIPPI: *Two panels: Annunciation.* New York, Frick Collection.

850. FRA FILIPPO LIPPI: *S. Augustine inspired by the Holy Trinity in his study (predella panel to the Barbadori Altarpiece).* Florence, Uffizi. *1437.*

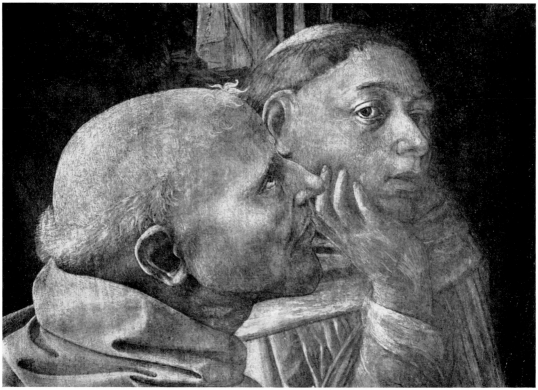

851–852. Fra Filippo Lippi: *Two details from the Coronation of the Virgin*. Florence, Uffizi. *1441*.

853. FRA FILIPPO LIPPI: *Madonna and Child.* Formerly New York, Carl Hamilton.

854. FRA FILIPPO LIPPI: *Madonna and Child.* Baltimore, Walters Art Gallery.

855. FRA FILIPPO LIPPI: *Annunciation.* Rome, Principe Doria Pamfili.

856. FRA FILIPPO LIPPI: *Tondo: Madonna and Child with Birth of Virgin in background.*
Florence, Pitti. *1452*

857. View of the Choir of the Duomo in Prato with frescoes by FRA FILIPPO LIPPI and his Assistants.
1456/66.

858. Fra Filippo Lippi: *Fresco: Presentation of the Head of the Baptist (detail).*
Prato, Duomo, Choir, Right Wall.

859. Fra Filippo Lippi: *Fresco: Leavetaking, Penitence and Preaching of the Baptist.*
Prato, Duomo, Choir, Right Wall.

860. Fra Filippo Lippi: *Fresco: Funeral of S. Stephen.* Prato, Duomo, Choir, Left Wall.
Signed and dated 1460.

861. Fra Filippo Lippi: *Madonna adoring the Child with S. Bernard and Infant S. John*
(commissioned by Lucrezia Tornabuoni). Florence, Uffizi. *ca 1463*.

862. FRA DIAMANTE (after Pesellino): *Madonna and Child.*
London, National Gallery.

863 a, b, c, d: FRA DIAMANTE: *Four Saints in niches from the frame of an altarpiece:* (a) formerly London,
Sir John Leslie; (b) and (c) Honolulu, Academy, Kress Collection; (d) New York, Robert Lehman.

864. Fra Filippo Lippi and Fra Diamante: *Madonna del Ceppo*. Prato, Pinacoteca. *1453*.

865. Fra Diamante on Fra Filippo's design: *Fresco: Nativity*. Spoleto, Duomo, Vault of Apse. *1467/69*.

866. FRA DIAMANTE: *Madonna and Child with SS. Lawrence, Anthony Abbot and a Donor.*
Budapest, Museum.

867. FRA DIAMANTE: *Predella panel: Circumcision.* Prato, Pinacoteca.

868–869. MASTER OF THE CASTELLO NATIVITY (?): *Two fresco lunettes: Miracle of the broken Sieve and Investiture of S. Benedict; S. Benedict in the Sacro Speco and the Priest at his Easter Meal.* Florence, Badia, Chiostro degli Aranci.

870. MASTER OF THE CASTELLO NATIVITY: *Profile portrait of Lady*. New York, Robert Lehman.

871. MASTER OF THE CASTELLO NATIVITY: *The Castello Nativity*. Florence, Accademia.

872–873. MASTER OF THE CASTELLO NATIVITY: *Madonna and Child against a portico*—Florence, Berenson Collection; *Madonna adoring the Child with Infant S. John*—Homeless.

874–875. MASTER OF THE CASTELLO NATIVITY: *Madonna and Child with Angels*—Paris, Louvre; *Madonna and Child*—Baltimore, Walters Art Gallery.

876. MASTER OF THE CASTELLO NATIVITY: *Madonna and Child with SS. Justus and Clement.*
Faltugnano, Pieve dei SS. Giusto e Clemente.

877. MASTER OF THE CASTELLO NATIVITY: *Predella panel to the Faltugnano Altarpiece: Multiplication of the Grain of Volterra by SS. Justus and Clement.* Philadelphia, Johnson Collection.

878. MASTER OF THE CASTELLO NATIVITY: *Annunciation*. Florence, S. Giovannino dei Cavalieri.

879. MASTER OF THE CASTELLO NATIVITY: *Predella panel to the Faltugnano Altarpiece: Nativity*.
London, National Gallery.

880. BENOZZO GOZZOLI: *Madonna and Child with nine Angels holding a Baldacchino.*
London, National Gallery.

881. BENOZZO GOZZOLI: *Birth and Marriage of the Virgin (detail from predella to Madonna della Cintola;*
from S. Fortunato in Montefalco). Rome, Pinacoteca Vaticana. *1450.*

882. BENOZZO GOZZOLI: *Fresco: S. Rose of Viterbo (detail).* Montefalco, S. Francesco,
Vault of Apse. *1452.*

883. BENOZZO GOZZOLI: *Frescoes: Trompe l'oeil polyptych: Madonna and Child with Saints, surrounded by
Crucifixion with four Saints; S. Jerome departing from Rome; S. Jerome and the Lion.*
Montefalco, S. Francesco, Cappella di S. Girolamo. *Signed and dated 1452.*

884. BENOZZO GOZZOLI: *Fresco: S. Francis receives the Homage of the Simpleton.* Montefalco, S. Francesco, Apse. *1452.*

885. BENOZZO GOZZOLI: *Fresco: S. Francis institutes the Presepio at Greccio.*
Montefalco, S. Francesco, Apse. *1452.*

886. BENOZZO GOZZOLI: *Fresco: Two Roundels with illustrious Franciscans.* Montefalco, S. Francesco.
1452.

887–888. BENOZZO GOZZOLI: *Frescoes: Shepherds guarding their flocks.* Florence, Palazzo Medici Riccardi.
1459.

889. BENOZZO GOZZOLI: *Fresco: The Journey of the Magi (detail)*. Florence, Palazzo Medici Riccardi. *1459*.

890. BENOZZO GOZZOLI: *Fresco: The Garden of Paradise (detail).* Florence, Palazzo Medici Riccardi. *1459.*

891. BENOZZO GOZZOLI: *Fresco: The Journey of the Magi (detail).* Florence, Palazzo Medici Riccardi. *1459.*

892. BENOZZO GOZZOLI: *Predella panel: Fall of Simon Magus*. London, Buckingham Palace. *1461*.
Reproduced by gracious permission of H.M. the Queen.

893. BENOZZO GOZZOLI: *Predella panel: S. Dominic raising a child*. Milan, Brera. *1461*.

894. BENOZZO GOZZOLI: *Fresco: S. Sebastian as Intercessor*. San Gimignano, S. Agostino. *Dated 1464.*

805. BENOZZO GOZZOLI: *Fresco: S. Augustine entrusted to his Tutor.* San Gimignano, S. Agostino. 1465.

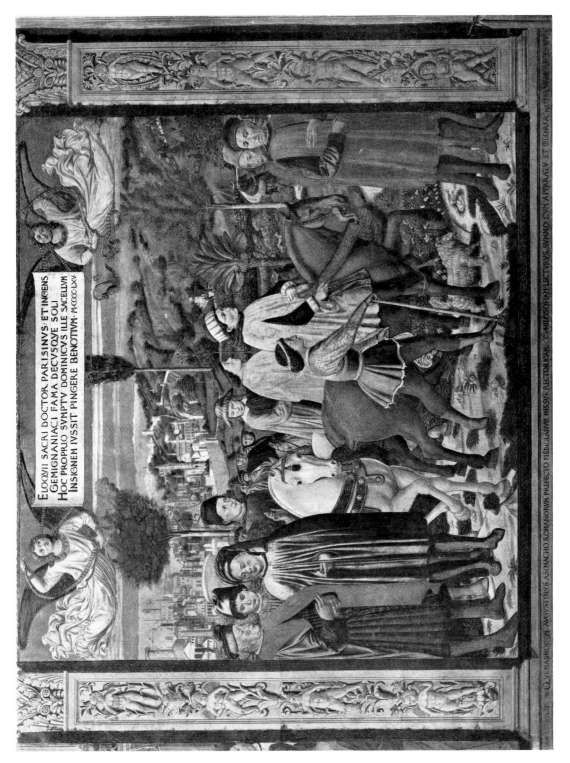

896. BENOZZO GOZZOLI: *Fresco: S. Augustine's Departure for Milan. San Gimignano, S. Agostino. Signed and dated 1465.*

897. BENOZZO GOZZOLI: *Marriage of S. Catherine with SS. Bartholomew, Francis and Lucy.*
Terni, Pinacoteca. *Signed and dated 1466.*

898–899. BENOZZO GOZZOLI: *Frescoes: Landscape detail from the Curse of Cam and detail from the Destruction of Sodom.* Pisa, Camposanto (destroyed). *1467/84.*

900. BENOZZO GOZZOLI: *Fresco: Construction of the Tower of Babel (detail)*. Pisa, Camposanto (destroyed). 1467/84.

902. BENOZZO GOZZOLI: *Madonna and Child with six Saints (detail)*.
Ottawa, National Gallery of Canada. *Dated 1473.*

901. BENOZZO GOZZOLI: *Fresco: The Drunkenness of Noah (detail)*.
Pisa, Camposanto (destroyed). *1467/84.*

904. Alunno di Benozzo: *Annunciation*. New York, Robert Lehman.

903. Alunno di Benozzo: *Madonna and Child with SS. Sebastian, Catherine, Ursula, Lawrence*. Florence, Bargello.

906. ALUNNO DI BENOZZO: *Lamentation*. Formerly Paris, Paul Delaroff.

905. ALUNNO DI BENOZZO: *Man of Sorrows*. Formerly Lyons, Aynard Collection.

907. Pier Francesco Fiorentino: *Madonna and Child with SS. Matthew, William, Barbara and Sebastian.* Empoli, Museo della Collegiata. *1474.*

908. Alunno di Benozzo: *Lamentation.* Florence, Mrs. C. H. Coster.

909. Amedo da Pistoia: *Madonna and Child with SS. Simon and Thaddeus.* Homeless. *Signed.*

910. PIER FRANCESCO FIORENTINO: *Madonna and Child with Tobias and the Angel, S. Anthony Abbot and a Bishop Saint.* Homeless. *Dated 1477.*

911. PIER FRANCESCO FIORENTINO: *Fresco: Incredulity of S. Thomas, with S. Jerome (detail).* Certaldo, Palazzo dei Priori. *Dated 1490.*

912. PIER FRANCESCO FIORENTINO: *Madonna and Child with eight Saints and donor;* in pilasters and predella, *Saints, Ascension, Man of Sorrows, Resurrection.* San Gimignano, S. Agostino. *Signed and dated 1494.*

913. NERI DI BICCI: *Madonna of Mercy with SS. Michael, Nicholas and Bernardino da Siena;*
in predella, *the Baptist, S. Bartholomew, Three Scenes illustrating the Destruction of the
Pagan Shrine at Fonte Tecta and the Founding of S. Maria delle Grazie by S. Bernardino.*
Arezzo, Pinacoteca. *Dated 1456.*

914. NERI DI BICCI: *Predella panel: Triumph of S. Michael.* Rotterdam, Boymans-Van Beuningen Museum.

915. Neri di Bicci: *Annunciation with S. Apollonia and S. Luke and the Prophets David and Isaiah.*
Florence, Accademia. *Dated 1458.*

916. Neri di Bicci: *Predella panel: S. Leonard praying for the safe delivery of a Queen.*
Florence, Serristori Collection.

917. NERI DI BICCI: *Madonna and Child with SS. James and Andrew.*
Homeless. *Dated 1463.*

918. NERI DI BICCI: *S. Felicitas and her seven sons.* Florence, S. Felicita.

919. NERI DI BICCI: *Annunciation*. Tavarnelle (Val di Pesa), S. Lucia al Borghetto. *Dated 1471*.

920. NERI DI BICCI: *Madonna adoring the Child with Infant S. John, surrounded by a cut-out Baldacchino.*
Barcelona, Museo.

921. NERI DI BICCI: *S. Anthony Abbot enthroned*. Denver, Museum of Art, Kress Collection.

922. NERI DI BICCI: *S. John Evangelist enthroned, with Tobias and the Angel, S. Lucy, S. William, and Annunciation above.* Homeless.

923. NERI DI BICCI: *S. Sebastian with SS. Bartholomew and Nicholas.* Volterra, Pinacoteca. *Dated 1478.*

924. GIUSTO D'ANDREA: *Madonna and Child with SS. Lawrence, Anthony Abbot, Julian, Lucy and John Gualbert.* Munich, Alte Pinakothek. *Dated 1458.*

925. GIUSTO D'ANDREA: *Madonna and Child with SS. Gregory, John Baptist, Francis and Fina.* San Gimignano, Palazzo Comunale.

926. Giusto d'Andrea: *S. Bonaventura with two Angels.*
Florence, S. Croce.

927. Giusto d'Andrea: *Madonna and Child with SS. John Baptist, Peter, Francis, Leonard and donor.*
Dijon, Musée.

928. VERROCCHIO: *Madonna and Child with two Angels*. London, National Gallery.

929. Verrocchio: *Madonna and Child*. Berlin, Staatliche Museen.

930. VERROCCHIO: *Marble Bust of Lady*. Florence, Bargello.

931. LEONARDO DA VINCI: *Bust of Ginevra dei Benci* (*fragment*). Vaduz, Liechtenstein Collection.

932. LEONARDO DA VINCI: *The Benois Madonna*. Leningrad, Hermitage.

933. LORENZO DI CREDI: *Madonna and Child with Infant S. John*. Dresden, Gemäldegalerie.

934. VERROCCHIO'S STUDIO: *Madonna of the Pomegranate*. Washington, National Gallery of Art, Kress Collection.

935. *The Pistoia Altarpiece*, commissioned from VERROCCHIO, executed by LORENZO DI CREDI under LEONARDO's influence: *Madonna and Child with SS. John Baptist and Donatus*. Pistoia, Duomo. *1478/85*.

936. LEONARDO DA VINCI and LORENZO DI CREDI: *Central panel of the predella to the Pistoia Altarpiece: Annunciation*. Paris, Louvre.

937. LEONARDO DA VINCI: *Detail from the Adoration of the Magi.* Florence, Uffizi. Commissioned in 1481 and left unfinished on leaving Florence in 1482.

938. PERUGINO (in VERROCCHIO's Studio): *Left panel of predella to the Pistoia Altarpiece: Birth of Baptist.* Liverpool, Walker Art Gallery.

939. LORENZO DI CREDI (in VERROCCHIO's Studio): *Right panel of predella to the Pistoia Altarpiece: S. Donatus and the Tax Collector (fragment).* Worcester (Mass.), Museum of Art.

940. Leonardo da Vinci: *The Virgin of the Rocks*. Paris, Louvre.

941. LORENZO DI CREDI: *Tondo: Madonna adoring the Child with Infant S. John.* Karlsruhe, Kunsthalle.

942. LORENZO DI CREDI: *Tondo: S. Lawrence in Glory*. San Marino (Cal.), Huntington Museum.

943. LORENZO DI CREDI: *Baptism of Christ* (imitating Verrocchio's and Leonardo's *Baptism*). Florence, S. Domenico di Fiesole.

944. LORENZO DI CREDI: *Last Communion of S. Mary Magdalen.*
Esztergom, Keresztény Múzeum.

945. LORENZO DI CREDI: *Young Woman
with pink sleeves.* Berlin, Staatliche Museen.

946. LORENZO DI CREDI: *Portrait of Verrocchio.*
Florence, Uffizi. *Before 1488.*

947. LORENZO DI CREDI: *Annunciation*. Florence, Uffizi.

949. LORENZO DI CREDI: *Noli me tangere* (*detail*).
Florence, Gallerie Fiorentine.

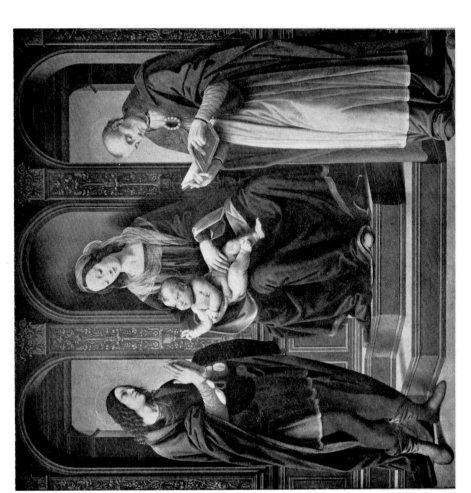

948. LORENZO DI CREDI: *Madonna and Child with SS. Julian and Nicholas*
(commissioned for Cestello in 1503). Paris, Louvre.

951. LORENZO DI CREDI: *S. Michael*. Florence, Duomo.
ca 1523.

950. LORENZO DI CREDI: *Adoration of the Shepherds, from S. Chiara (detail)*.
Florence, Uffizi. 1510.

953. Florentine Follower of LEONARDO: *Madonna and Child.*
Berlin, Staatliche Museen. (Destroyed).

952. Florentine Follower of LEONARDO: *Madonna with the two Holy Children.*
Florence, Poggio a Caiano, Villa Medicea (Gallerie Fiorentine).

955. DOMENICO GHIRLANDAJO: *Madonna and Child*. Washington, National Gallery of Art, Kress Collection.

954. DOMENICO GHIRLANDAJO: *Madonna and Child*. Paris, Louvre.

957. DOMENICO GHIRLANDAJO: *Fresco lunette: Madonna of Mercy with the Vespucci Family (detail).* Florence, Ognissanti.

956. DOMENICO GHIRLANDAJO: *Fragment of Nativity: Virgin adoring.* Formerly London, W. H. Woodward.

958. DOMENICO GHIRLANDAJO: *Fresco: S. Fina receiving from S. Gregory the news of her approaching death. San Gimignano, Collegiata, Cappella di S. Fina. ca 1475.*

959. DOMENICO GHIRLANDAJO: *Fresco: Last Supper (detail)*.
Florence, Convento di S. Marco, Small Refectory.

960. DOMENICO GHIRLANDAJO: *Fresco: Last Supper*. Florence, Ognissanti, Refectory. *Dated 1480.*

961. DOMENICO GHIRLANDAJO: *Fresco: Glory of S. Zenobius (detail of Madonna in lunette).*
Florence, Palazzo Vecchio, Sala dei Gigli. *1482/84.*

962. DOMENICO GHIRLANDAJO: *The Meeting of Jesus and the young S. John in the Wilderness.*
Berlin, Staatliche Museen.

963. DOMENICO and DAVIDE GHIRLANDAJO with Assistants: *Frescoes: Glory of S. Zenobius, Roman Heroes.*
Florence, Palazzo Vecchio, Sala dei Gigli. *1482/84.*

964. DOMENICO GHIRLANDAJO and Assistants: *Fresco: Vocation of SS. Peter and Andrew.*
Rome, Vatican, Cappella Sistina. *1482.*

965. View of the Cappella Sassetti with frescoes and altarpiece by DOMENICO GHIRLANDAJO. Florence, S. Trinita. *1485*.

966. DOMENICO GHIRLANDAJO: *Fresco: Approval of the Franciscan Order (detail of Angelo Poliziano and his pupil Giuliano de' Medici).* Florence, S. Trinita, Cappella Sassetti. *1485.*

967. DOMENICO GHIRLANDAJO: *Adoration of the Magi* (in background, *Massacre of Innocents* by Bartolomeo di Giovanni). Florence, Spedale degli Innocenti. *1488.*

968, 969. DOMENICO GHIRLANDAJO and Assistants: *Frescoes: Visitation, Birth of the Virgin*. Florence, S. Maria Novella, Choir. *1486/90*.

970, 971. DOMENICO GHIRLANDAJO and Assistants: *Baptism of Christ, Annunciation to Zacharias* (dated *1490*). Florence, S. Maria Novella, Choir. *1486/90*.

973. MAINARDI: S. Stephen (part of
S. Maria Novella Altarpiece).

972. DAVIDE GHIRLANDAJO and GRANACCI: Resurrection (back panel of S. Maria Novella Altarpiece).
Berlin, Staatliche Museen. Soon after 1494.

975. GRANACCI: *S. Vincent (part of S. Maria Novella Altarpiece).* Berlin, Staatliche Museen. *Soon after 1494.*

974. GRANACCI and MAINARDI ON DOMENICO GHIRLANDAJO's design: *Madonna in Glory with SS. Dominic, Michael, John Baptist and John Evangelist (front panel of S. Maria Novella Altarpiece).* Munich, Alte Pinakothek. *Soon after 1494.*

976. Domenico Ghirlandajo and Mainardi: *Visitation
with SS. Mary of James and Mary Salome*. Paris, Louvre. *Dated 1491*.

977. Mainardi: *Fresco: Annunciation*. San Gimignano, Collegiata, Oratorio di S. Giovanni.
Dated 1482.

978. MAINARDI: *S. Barbara and a donor*. Balcarres, Earl of Crawford and Balcarres.

979. MAINARDI: *Tondo: Madonna and Child with Infant S. John.*
Maidenhead, Sir Thomas Merton.

980. MAINARDI: *The Rosary: Male Worshippers.* Philadelphia (Pa.), Johnson Collection.

981. MAINARDI: *Tondo: Adoration of the Shepherds*. Homeless.
Dated 1493

982. MAINARDI: *The Rosary: Female Worshippers*. Philadelphia (Pa.), Johnson Collection.

984. MAINARDI: *Frescoed Tabernacle: Nativity, S. Ansanus and S. Roch,*
Florence, Brozzi.

983. MAINARDI: *Fresco: Madonna della Cintola.* Florence, S. Croce,
Cappella Baroncelli.

986. MAINARDI: *Tondo: Nativity with Infant S. John (detail)*. Homeless.

985. MAINARDI: *Madonna adoring the Child*. Homeless.

987, 988. DAVIDE (and BENEDETTO?) GHIRLANDAJO: *Fresco lunettes: Visiting Prisoners, Giving Drink to the Thirsty.* Florence, S. Martino Buonomini. *After 1479.*

989. DAVIDE GHIRLANDAJO: *Fresco lunette: Brutus, Mucius Scaevola and Camillus.* Florence, Palazzo Vecchio. *1482/84.* (See Pl. 963).

990. DAVIDE GHIRLANDAJO: *Fresco: Madonna and Child with Angels and donor.* Stia, S. Maria delle Grazie. *Dated 1485.*

991. DAVIDE GHIRLANDAJO: *Mosaic: Madonna and Child and Angels.* Paris, Musée de Cluny. *Formerly signed and dated 1496.*

993. DAVIDE GHIRLANDAJO: *Bust of Woman*. Altenburg, Lindenau Museum.

992. BENEDETTO GHIRLANDAJO: *Bust of Woman*. Balmville (Newburgh, N.Y.), Miss Tessie Jones.

995. BENEDETTO GHIRLANDAJO (?): *Nativity*. Philadelphia, Johnson Collection.

994. DAVIDE GHIRLANDAJO: *Judith*. Berlin, Staatliche Museen. *Dated 1489.*

996. BENEDETTO AND DAVIDE GHIRLANDAJO: *S. Lucy and donor.*
Florence, S. Maria Novella. *1494.*

997. BENEDETTO GHIRLANDAJO: *Predella panel: S. Vincent Ferrer raising a child on an altar.*
Florence, Museo Stibbert.

998. BENEDETTO GHIRLANDAJO: *Nativity*. Aigueperse, Notre-Dame. *Signed.*

999. COSIMO ROSSELLI: *Adoration of the Magi.* Florence, Gallerie Fiorentine.

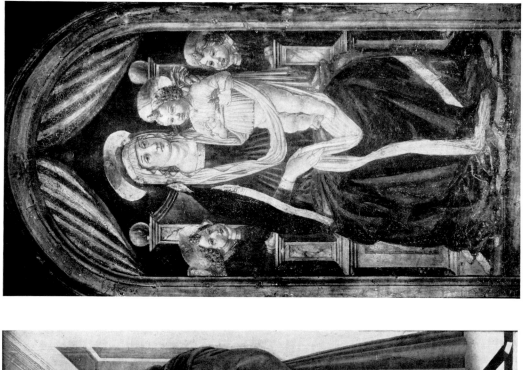

1001. COSIMO ROSSELLI: *Tabernacle Fresco: Madonna and Child with two Angels.* Florence, via Ricasoli.

1000. COSIMO ROSSELLI: *Madonna and Child with S. Anne and SS. George, Catherine, Mary Magdalen and Francis.* Berlin, Staatliche Museen. *Dated 1471.*

1002. Cosimo Rosselli: *Madonna and Child in Glory* (*fragment*).
San Marino (Cal.), Huntington Museum.

1003, 1004. Cosimo Rosselli: *Two Innocents*
(*fragments*). Homeless.

1005. Cosimo Rosselli: *S. Lucy*
(*fragment*). Homeless.

1006. COSIMO ROSSELLI: *Fresco: Vocation of Blessed Philip Benizzi.* Florence, SS. Annunziata.
1476.

1007. COSIMO ROSSELLI: *Fresco: Last Supper (the scenes in the windows, by 'Utili').* Rome, Vatican,
Cappella Sistina. *1482.*

1008. COSIMO ROSSELLI: *Fresco:*
Detail from the Sermon on the Mount.
Rome, Cappella Sistina. *1482.*

1009. COSIMO ROSSELLI: *Portrait of*
Matteo Sassetti. New York, Jack Linsky.

1010. COSIMO ROSSELLI: *Fresco: Miracle of the Holy Blood.* Florence, S. Ambrogio, Cappella del Miracolo.
1486.

1011. COSIMO ROSSELLI: *Fresco: Miracle of the Holy Blood* (*detail*). Florence, S. Ambrogio,
Cappella del Miracolo. *1486*.

1012. COSIMO ROSSELLI: *Disrobing of Christ, Way to Calvary*. Formerly London, Henry Harris.

1013. COSIMO ROSSELLI: *Predella panel: Annunciation*. Gazzada, Villa Cagnola.

1014. COSIMO ROSSELLI: *Portable altarpiece: Madonna della Cintola*. London, Sir Thomas Barlow.

1015. COSIMO ROSSELLI: *The Triumph of Chastity*. Turin, Galleria Sabauda.

1016. COSIMO ROSSELLI: *The Daughters of Jephta*. Formerly London, J. S. Maynard.

1017. COSIMO ROSSELLI: *Madonna and Child with an Angel*. Upton House, National Trust.

1018. COSIMO ROSSELLI: *Tondo: Madonna adoring the Child with Infant S. John*. Homeless.

1019. COSIMO ROSSELLI: *Madonna and Child with Cherubim*. Homeless.

1020. COSIMO ROSSELLI: *Madonna and Child in Glory (fragment)*. Homeless.

1021. Cosimo Rosselli: *Prophet* in interstice beside pinnacle of Lorenzo Monaco's *Adoration of Magi.*
Florence, Uffizi.

1022. COSIMO ROSELLI: *Madonna and Child with Infant S. John, S. James and S. Peter.*
Florence, Uffizi. *1492.*

1023. COSIMO ROSSELLI: *Altarpiece from Radda: Madonna and Child with S. Euphrosynus, S. John Baptist and Bartolomeo Canigiani as Donor;* in predella, *Nativity, Baptism of Christ and Death of S. Euphrosynus.* Florence, Palazzo Vecchio.

1024. Florentine between CosIMO ROSSELLI and PIERO DI CosIMO: *Tondo: Holy Family with Infant S. John*. Formerly Florence, Fairfax Murray.

1025. Florentine between PIERO DI COSIMO, RAFFAELLINO DEL GARBO and GRANACCI: *Tondo: Holy Family with Infant S. John*. Formerly Paris, Eugène Richtemberger.

1026. 'UTILI': *Madonna adoring the Child with an Angel.*
New York, Samuel H. Kress Foundation.

1027. 'UTILI': *Cassone panel with Story of Joseph (detail)*. New York, Metropolitan Museum.

1028. 'UTILI': *Madonna and Child with SS. Peter Martyr, Catherine of Siena, Vincent Ferrer, James, and a Bishop Saint.* Budapest, Museum.

1029. 'UTILI': *Detail of the Three Archangels with Tobias.* Florence, Bartolini Salimbeni Collection. *After 1461 and before 1471, as the Cupola of the Duomo of Florence is shown without Verrocchio's gilt-bronze ball.*

1030. 'UTILI': *The Three Archangels with Tobias*. Florence, Bartolini Salimbeni Collection. *1461/1471*.

1031. 'UTILI': *The Nerli Cassone*. London, Courtauld Galleries, Lee of Fareham Collection. *1472*.

1032. 'UTILI': Cassone panel: Story of Joseph. Homeless.

1033. 'UTILI': Cassone panel: Story of the Argonauts. New York, Metropolitan Museum.

1034. 'UTILI': *Cassone panel: Triumphal Procession (detail).*
Washington, National Gallery of Art, Kress Collection.

1035. 'UTILI': *Cassone panel: Story of Lucretia (detail).* Venice, Ca'd'Oro.

1036. 'UTILI': *Fresco: Detail from the Crossing of the Red Sea.* Rome, Vatican, Cappella Sistina. *1482.*

1037. DAVIDE GHIRLANDAJO and 'UTILI': *Fresco: The Crossing of the Red Sea*. Rome, Vatican, Cappella Sistina. *1482*.

1039. 'UTILI': *Madonna and Child*. Homeless.

1038. 'UTILI': *Madonna and Child with Angel*. Milan, Museo Poldi Pezzoli.

1040. 'UTILI': *Crucifixion*. Oxford, Christ Church Library.

1041. 'UTILI': *Triptych: Madonna and Child with two Angels; SS. Dominic, Andrew, John Evangelist and Thomas Aquinas; in lunette, Annunciation.* Faenza, Pinacoteca. *1483.*

1042. 'UTILI': *The Demidoff Tondo: Madonna and Child with two Angels.*
Formerly Belgrade, Royal Palace.

1043. 'UTILI': *Madonna and Child with SS. Francis, Benedict(?), Louis of Toulouse, Lucy, Bernardo degli Uberti*
and Anthony of Padua (detail). Bremen, Kunsthalle.

1044. 'Utili': *Way to Calvary*. Paris, Louvre.

1045. MASTER OF S. MINIATO: *Madonna and Child with SS. John Baptist, Clement, Bartholomew and Anthony Abbot.* Gaviserri, S. Andrea Corsini.

1046. MASTER OF S. MINIATO: *Predella panel: Burial of S. Catherine of Siena.* Pittsfield (Mass.), Mrs. Lawrence K. Miller.

1047. MASTER OF S. MINIATO: *Madonna and Child with SS. Sebastian and Romuald (detail)*.
Pomino (Pontassieve), Chiesa Parrocchiale.

1048. MASTER OF S. MINIATO: *Predella panel: Legend of S. Barbara*. Rome, Pinacoteca Vaticana.

1049 MASTER OF S. MINIATO: *Madonna and Child with SS. Sebastian, John Baptist, Roch and a Bishop Saint, and the donor with his wife and child*. San Miniato al Tedesco, S. Domenico.

1050. MASTER OF S. MINIATO: *Madonna and Child*
with SS. Francis and Julian. Homeless.

1051. MASTER OF S. MINIATO: *Madonna and Child*
with two Angels. Formerly New York, W. R. Hearst.

1052. MASTER OF S. MINIATO: *SS. Cosmas, Lucy and Damian (detail of Madonna in Glory with Saints)*.
San Miniato al Tedesco, Cappella della Misericordia.

1053. MASTER OF S. MINIATO: *S. Nicholas enthroned with SS. Apollonia, Margaret, Lucy and Catherine.* Formerly, London, W. H. Woodward.

1054. MASTER OF S. MINIATO: *Deposition.* Paris, Musées Nationaux (from Lyons).

1055. MASTER OF S. MINIATO: *Madonna and Child with S. James and an Evangelist.*
London, Peter Harris.

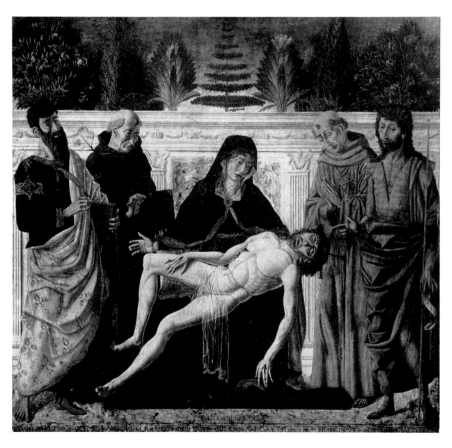

1056. MASTER OF S. MINIATO(?): *Lamentation with SS. Bartholomew, Nicholas of Tolentino,*
Francis and John Baptist. Arundel Castle, Duke of Norfolk. *Dated 1460.*

1057. Florentine close to BOTTICINI: *Madonna and Child with SS. Mary Magdalen, John Baptist, Anthony Abbot and Francis*. Romena, Pieve di S. Pietro.

1058. BOTTICINI: *Madonna and Child with SS. John Baptist, Pancras, Sebastian and Peter*. Paris, Musée Jacquemart-André. *Dated 1471*.

1059. BOTTICINI: *Madonna and Child with two Angels and SS. Benedict, Francis, Silvester and Anthony Abbot.* Homeless.

1060. BOTTICINI: *Matteo Palmieri before a view of Florence (detail of Assumption).* London, National Gallery. *Before 1475.*

1061. BOTTICINI: *The Palmieri Assumption (detail)*. London, National Gallery.

1063. BOTTICINI: *Tobias and the Angel with a young donor.*
Florence, Accademia.

1062. BOTTICINI: *The three Archangels with Tobias (detail).*
Florence, Uffizi.

1064. BOTTICINI: *Madonna and Child in Glory with SS. Mary of Egypt and Bernard*. Paris, Louvre.

1065. BOTTICINI: *Madonna and Child with Tobias and the Angel, S. Francis and a female donor.* Balcarres, Earl of Crawford and Balcarres.

1066. BOTTICINI: *Crucifixion with SS. Anthony Abbot, Lawrence, Peter Martyr, Tobias and the Angel.* Berlin, Staatliche Museen. *Dated 1475.*

1067. BOTTICINI: *Tondo: Madonna adoring the Child with Infant S. John.*
Formerly Ashburnham Place, Lady Ashburnham.

1068. BOTTICINI: *The 'Panciatichi and Benson' Tondo: Madonna and Child.*
Cincinnati (Ohio), Art Museum.

1069. BOTTICINI: *S. Monica with Augustinian Nuns and two worshipping girls;* in predella, *Life of S. Monica.*
Florence, S. Spirito. (*1483?*).

1070. BOTTICINI: *Feast of Herod (detail from the predella to the Tabernacle of the Holy Sacrament).*
Empoli, Museo della Collegiata. *1484/91.*

1071. BOTTICELLI: *Madonna and Child with an Angel*. Ajaccio, Musée Fesch.

1072. BOTTICELLI: *Madonna and Child*. Paris, Louvre.

1073. BOTTICELLI: *Predella panel: Annunciation*. Glens Falls (N.Y.), Mrs. Louis Hyde.

1074. BOTTICELLI: *S. Sebastian.* Berlin, Staatliche Museen. *1473/74.*

1075. Botticelli: *Judith*. Florence, Uffizi.

1076. Botticelli: *Predella panel: Noli me tangere*. Philadelphia, Johnson Collection.

1077. BOTTICELLI: *The 'Medici' Adoration of the Magi*. Florence, Uffizi.

1079. Botticelli: *Detail from 'La Primavera'.* Florence, Uffizi. ca 1478/80.

1078. Botticelli: *Portrait of Giuliano de' Medici.* Washington, National Gallery, Kress Collection.

1080. BOTTICELLI: *Fresco: Detail from Annunciation.* Florence, S. Martino alla Scala. *1481.*

1081. BOTTICELLI: *Fresco: Detail from the Purification of the Leper*. Rome, Vatican, Cappella Sistina. *1482*.

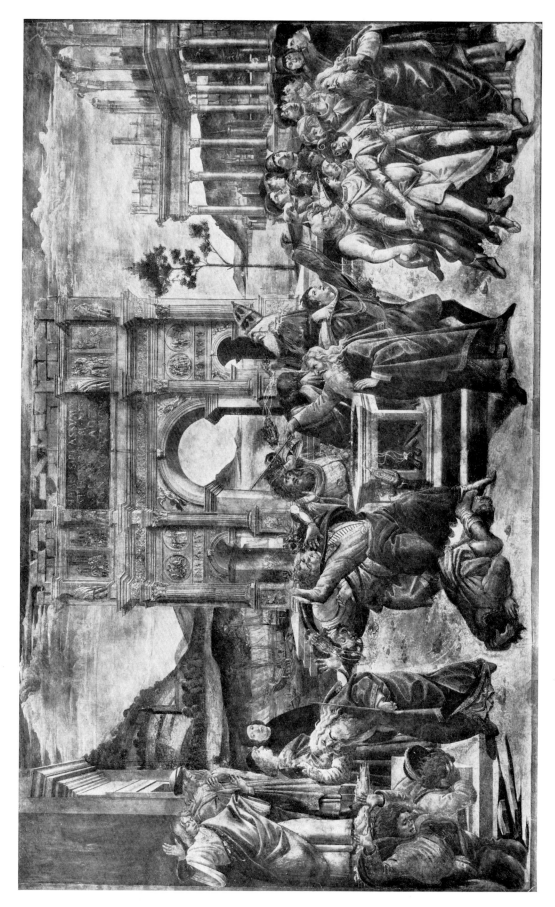

1082. BOTTICELLI: *Fresco: Destruction of the Children of Korah.* Rome, Vatican, Cappella Sistina. 1482.

1084. BOTTICELLI: *Head of the Baptist in the S. Barnaba altarpiece (plate 1085).*
Florence, Uffizi.

1083. BOTTICELLI: *Portrait of a Monk as Saint Augustine.*
Zurich, Annie Abegg-Stockar.

1085. BOTTICELLI: *Madonna and Child with four Angels and SS. Catherine, Augustine, Barnabas, John Baptist, Ignatius and Michael* (from the Church of S. Barnaba). Florence, Uffizi.

1086. BOTTICELLI: *Tondo: Madonna of the Pomegranate*. Florence, Uffizi. *1487*.

1087. BOTTICELLI: *Last Communion of S. Jerome.*
New York, Metropolitan Museum.

1088. BOTTICELLI: *Annunciation.* New York, Robert Lehman.

1089. BOTTICELLI: *Tondo: Madonna and Child with three Angels.*
Milan, Ambrosiana.

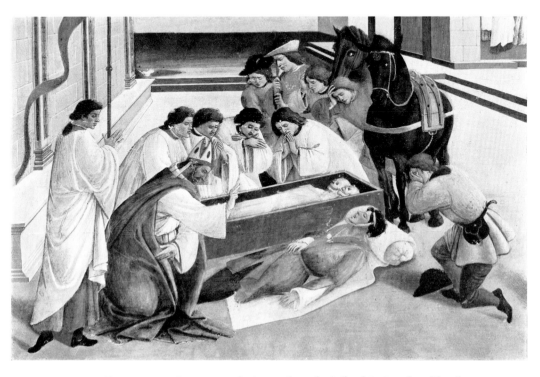

1090. BOTTICELLI: *Cassone panel: Scenes from the Life of S. Zenobius (detail).*
New York, Metropolitan Museum.

1092. BOTTICELLI: *La Calunnia* (*detail*). Florence, Uffizi.

1091. BOTTICELLI: *Judith*. Amsterdam, Rijksmuseum.

1093. BOTTICELLI: *Cassone panel: Story of Virginia.* Bergamo, Accademia Carrara. *ca 1499.*

1096. BOTTICELLI: *Mystic Crucifixion*. Cambridge (Mass.), Fogg Art Museum.

1095. BOTTICELLI: *Agony in the Garden*. Granada, Capilla Real.

1096. BOTTICELLI: *Mystic Nativity (detail)*. London, National Gallery. *Signed and dated 1500.*

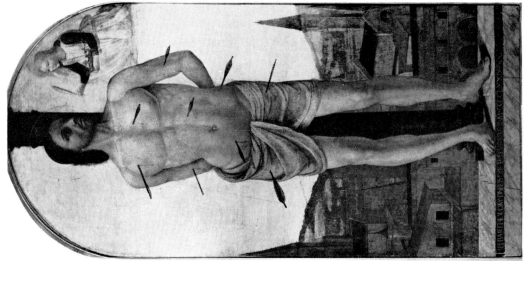

1098. SELLAJO: S. Sebastian. New Haven (Conn.),
Yale University. Dated 1479.

1097. SELLAJO: *Annunciation;* in predella, *Nativity, SS. Martin and Sebastian.*
San Giovanni Valdarno, Museo. Dated 1472.

1099. SELLAJO: *A Wilderness with S. Jerome, Job, the Meeting of Jesus and S. John Baptist, the penitent Magdalen.* Milan, Contessa Rasini.

1100. SELLAJO: *Pietà with S. Jerome and a Bishop Saint*. Berlin, Staatliche Museen. (Destroyed). *ca 1483*.

1101. SELLAJO: *Man of Sorrows*. Homeless.

1102. SELLAJO: *Christ on the Cross with SS. Frediano, Catherine, the Virgin, S. John Evangelist, Sebastian, Tobias and the Angel, Mary Magdalen, and Lawrence*. Florence, S. Frediano.

1103. SELLAJO: *Pietà*. Leningrad, Hermitage.

1105. SELLAJO: *Cassone panel: Story of Cupid and Psyche (left half)*. Amsterdam, E. Proehl.

1104. SELLAJO: *Tondo: Madonna adoring the Child with Infant S. John.* Florence, Pitti.

1106. SELLAJO: *Cassone panel: Story of Cupid and Psyche (right half).* Amsterdam, E. Proehl.

1107–1108. SELLAJO: *Two details from cassone panel with Story of Orpheus and Eurydice.* Kiev, Museum.

1109. SELLAJO: *The young S. John Baptist, Patron Saint of Florence.*
Washington, National Gallery, Kress Collection.

1110. SELLAJO: *Cassone panel: Julius Caesar being warned before his murder.* Berlin, Staatliche Museen.

1112. SELLAJO: *The Redeemer*. Birmingham (Ala.), Museum of Art, Kress Collection.

1111. BOTTICELLI: *The Redeemer*. Bergamo, Accademia Carrara.

1114. SELLAJO: *Madonna and Child*. Florence, Galleria Corsini.

1113. BOTTICELLI: *Madonna and Child with S. John Baptist and S. John Evangelist (detail)*.
Berlin, Staatliche Museen. 1484/85.

1115. Botticelli and Bartolomeo di Giovanni: *Banquet of Nastagio degli Onesti*. Madrid, Prado. *1483*.

1116. Bartolomeo di Giovanni: *Martyrdom of S. Sebastian (from predella to altarpiece by Domenico Ghirlandajo)*. Lucca, Duomo, Sacristy. *ca 1485*.

1117. BARTOLOMEO DI GIOVANNI: *Cassone panel: Banquet of the Argonauts in Colchis.*
Formerly Cape Town, Sir Joseph Robinson Collection. *ca 1487.*

1118–19. BARTOLOMEO DI GIOVANNI: *Circumcision, Baptism (from predella to Domenico Ghirlandajo's Adoration of Magi).* Florence, Spedale degli Innocenti. *1488.*

1121. Bartolomeo di Giovanni: *Cassone panel: Myth of Io (detail)*. Baltimore, Walters Art Gallery.

1120. Bartolomeo di Giovanni: *Cassone panel: Rape of Sabines (detail)*. Rome, Galleria Colonna.

1122. BARTOLOMEO DI GIOVANNI: *Cassone panel: Myth of Io.* Berchtesgaden, Schloss.

1123. BARTOLOMEO DI GIOVANNI: *Cassone panel: Triumph of Thetis.* Paris, Louvre.

1125. BARTOLOMEO DI GIOVANNI: *Flagellation*. Bergamo, Accademia Carrara.

1124. BARTOLOMEO DI GIOVANNI: *Predella panel: S. Benedict blessing the poisoned wine.*
Florence, Uffizi.

1127. Bartolomeo di Giovanni: *The penitent S. Jerome.* Palermo, Chiaramonte Bordonaro Collection.

1126. Bartolomeo di Giovanni: *Madonna adoring the Child with Infant S. John.* Aix-en-Provence, Musée Granet.

1128. BARTOLOMEO DI GIOVANNI: *The 'Wittgenstein' Tondo: Adoration of the Magi.*
San Francisco (Cal.), De Young Memorial Museum, Kress Collection.

1129. BARTOLOMEO DI GIOVANNI: *Predella panel: S. Andrew saving a Bishop from seduction.*
Liverpool, Walker Art Gallery.

1130. BARTOLOMEO DI GIOVANNI: *Crucifixion with SS. Monica, Augustine, Mary Magdalen, Jerome and a female Saint*. Formerly Parcieux, Georges Chalandon.

1131. BARTOLOMEO DI GIOVANNI: *Lamentation with Saints and a donor*. Formerly Florence, Marchese Mannelli Riccardi.

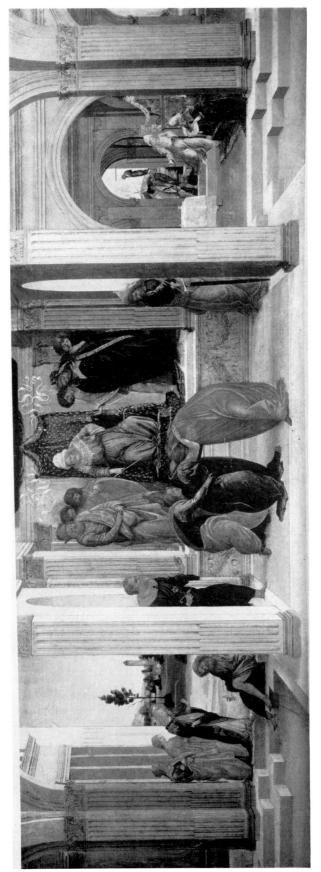

1132. FILIPPINO LIPPI: *Cassone panel: The Swooning of Esther and the Revocation of the Edict against the Jews*. Paris, Comtesse de Vogüé.

1133–34. FILIPPINO LIPPI: *Cassone panels: Esther arriving at Susa, Triumph of Mordecai*. Ottawa, National Gallery of Canada.

1135. FILIPPINO LIPPI: *Coronation of the Virgin*. Washington, National Gallery of Art, Kress Collection.

1136. FILIPPINO LIPPI: *Madonna and Child with a Book*.
Berlin, Staatliche Museen.

1137. FILIPPINO LIPPI: *Tondo: Madonna adoring the Child with six Angels (detail)*. Leningrad, Hermitage.

1138. FILIPPINO LIPPI: *Allegory of Love*. Milan, Contessa Rasini.

1139. FILIPPINO LIPPI: *Fresco: Detail of Bystanders in The Raising of the Son of Theophilus.*
Florence, S. Maria del Carmine, Cappella Brancacci.

1140. FILIPPINO LIPPI: *Fresco: Crucifixion of S. Peter*. Florence, S. Maria del Carmine,
Cappella Brancacci.

1141. FILIPPINO LIPPI: *Fresco: Self-portrait (detail from Plate 1142).*

ILIPPINO LIPPI: *Fresco: SS. Peter and Paul before the Proconsul.* Florence, S. Maria del Carmine,
Cappella Brancacci.

1144. FILIPPINO LIPPI: *The Donor Piero di Francesco del Pugliese,
in the Vision of S. Bernard.* Florence, Badia.

1143. FILIPPINO LIPPI: *Fresco: Liberation of S. Peter (detail).*
Florence, Carmine, Cappella Brancacci.

1145, 1146. FILIPPINO LIPPI: *Two Tondi: Annunciation.* San Gimignano, Museo. *1483/84.*

1147. FILIPPINO LIPPI: *Altarpiece from the Office of the 'Otto di Pratica' in Palazzo Vecchio: Madonna and Child with SS. John Baptist, Victor, Bernard and Zenobius.* Florence, Uffizi. *Dated 1485.*

1148. FILIPPINO LIPPI and Assistants: *Fresco lunette: The Miracle of the Crucifix at Naples.*
Rome, S. Maria sopra Minerva, Cappella Caraffa. *1489/93.*

1149. FILIPPINO LIPPI: *Madonna and Child with Infant S. John, SS. Martin and Catherine and Tanai de'Nerli and his wife as donors (view of Porta S. Frediano in background).*
Florence, S. Spirito.

1150. FILIPPINO LIPPI: *The 'Warren' Tondo: Holy Family with Infant S. John and S. Margaret.*
Cleveland, Museum of Art.

1151. FILIPPINO LIPPI: *Meeting at the Golden Gate.* Copenhagen, Royal Museum.
Signed and dated 1497.

1152. FILIPPINO LIPPI: *Frescoes: 'Tabernacolo del Canto a Mercatale': Madonna and Child with Seraphim, SS. Anthony Abbot and Margaret, SS. Stephen and Catherine*. Prato, Pinacoteca. *Dated 1498.*

1153. FILIPPINO LIPPI: *Allegory of Music*. Berlin, Staatliche Museen.

1154. FILIPPINO LIPPI: *Fresco: S. Philip exorcizing in the Temple of Hieropolis (detail).* Florence, S. Maria Novella, Cappella di Filippo Strozzi. *ca 1502.*

1155. RAFFAELLINO: *Madonna and Child with Angels and SS. Bartholomew, Nicholas and two donors.*
Florence, S. Spirito.

1156. RAFFAELLINO: *Cassone panel with Story of Susanna (detail).* Baltimore, Walters Art Gallery.

1157. RAFFAELLINO: *Tondo: Madonna and Child with two music-making Angels.*
Berlin, Staatliche Museen.

1158. RAFFAELLINO: *The 'Benson' Tondo: Madonna and Child with two Angels
and Infant S. John.* Formerly New York, W. R. Hearst.

1159. RAFFAELLINO: *S. Mary Magdalen.* Oxford, Christ Church Library.

1160. RAFFAELLINO: *Profile portrait of woman.* Paris, E. de Rothschild.

1161. RAFFAELLINO: *Resurrection (for Niccolò Capponi).* Florence, Accademia.

1162. RAFFAELLINO: *Madonna and Child with Infant S. John.*
Berlin, Dr. P. Bonn.

1163. RAFFAELLINO: *Lamentation with SS. John Baptist and James.* Munich, Alte Pinakothek.

1164. RAFFAELLINO: *Tondo (detached fresco): Madonna and Child.*
Formerly Chilston Park (Kent), Viscountess Chilston.

1165. RAFFAELLINO: *'Pucci' Tondo: Madonna and Child with SS. Mary Magdalen
and Catherine.* London, National Gallery.

1166. RAFFAELLINO: *Madonna and Child with SS. Francis, Zenobius, a donor and his wife.*
Florence, Gallerie Fiorentine. *Signed and dated 1500.*

1167. RAFFAELLINO: *Tondo: Madonna and Child between S. Jerome and S. Francis.* Homeless.

1168. RAFFAELLINO: *The 'Corsini' Altarpiece: Madonna and Child with two Angels, SS. Jerome and Bartholomew.*
San Francisco (Cal.), De Young Memorial Museum, Kress Collection. *Signed and dated 1502.*

1169. RAFFAELLINO: *Tondo: Madonna and Child with Infant S. John and Angels.*
Formerly Beverley Hills, Miss Marion Davies.

1170. RAFFAELLINO: *Detail of predella: Stoning of S. Stephen.* Florence, S. Spirito. *1505.*

1171. RAFFAELLINO: *S. John Gualbert with SS. Mary Magdalen, John Baptist, Bernardo degli Uberti and Catherine.* Vallombrosa, Abbazia. *Dated 1508.*

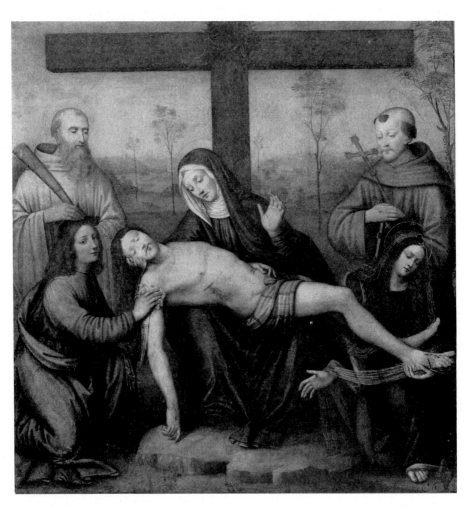

1172. RAFFAELLINO: *Pietà with SS. Benedict and Francis.* Formerly Olantigh Towers, Mr. Sawbridge Erle Drax.

1173. Master of the Lathrop Tondo: *Tondo: Madonna and Child with SS. Jerome, Catherine and donor*. Formerly New York, Francis Lathrop.

1174. MASTER OF THE LATHROP TONDO: *SS. Jerome and Joseph*

1175. MASTER OF THE LATHROP TONDO: *Wings of altarpiece: S. Blaise with male donor;*

1177. MASTER OF THE LATHROP TONDO: *Madonna della Cintola.*
Sarasota (Fla.), Ringling Museum.

1176. MASTER OF THE LATHROP TONDO: *Madonna and Child with SS. Augustine,
Monica, Anthony of Padua and Jerome.* Lucca, Pinacoteca.

1178. 'TOMMASO': *Madonna and Child with Angel*. Santa Monica (Cal.), Paul J. Getty Museum.

1179. 'TOMMASO': *Tondo: Madonna and Child with Angel and Infant S. John.*
Homeless.

1180. 'TOMMASO': *Tondo: Madonna adoring the Child with two Angels and Infant S. John.*
Los Angeles (Cal.), County Museum.

1181. 'TOMMASO': *Cassone panel: Venus asks Cupid to wound Adonis with the arrows of Love.* Edenbridge (Kent), Archibald Werner.

1182. 'TOMMASO': *Large Pietà*. Formerly Nijmegen, H. W. Jurgens.

1183. 'TOMMASO': *Tondo: Madonna and Child with two music-making Angels.*
Leningrad, Hermitage.

1184. 'TOMMASO': *Predella panel: Martyrdom of S. Sebastian.* Milan, Museo Poldi Pezzoli.

1185. 'TOMMASO': *Madonna and Child with SS. John Evangelist and Jerome (after the Pistoia altarpiece—see pl. 935)*. Florence, S. Spirito.

1186. 'TOMMASO': *Predella panel: Nativity*. Bergamo, Accademia Carrara.

1187. PIERO DI COSIMO: *Tondo: Holy Family with two reading Angels and Infant S. John.*
Dresden, Gemäldegalerie.

1188. Piero di Cosimo: *Cassone panel: Venus, Cupid and Mars (detail)*. Berlin, Staatliche Museen.

1189. PIERO DI COSIMO: *Cassone panel: Venus, Cupid and Mars (detail)*. Berlin, Staatliche Museen.

1190. PIERO DI COSIMO: *Cassone panel: Fight between Centaurs and Lapiths (detail)*. London, National Gallery.

1191. Piero di Cosimo: *Adoration of the Shepherds*. Berlin, Staatliche Museen. (Destroyed).

1193. PIERO DI COSIMO: *Madonna and Child with book and dove.*
Paris, Louvre.

1192. PIERO DI COSIMO: *Madonna and Child reading a book* (after Filippino Lippi).
Stockholm, Royal Palace.

1194. PIERO DI COSIMO: *Portrait of the architect Francesco Giamberti, father of Giuliano da San Gallo.*
Amsterdam, Rijksmuseum.

1195. PIERO DI COSIMO: *Vulcan and Aeolus (detail)*. Ottawa, National Gallery of Canada.

1106. Piero di Cosimo: *The Hunt* (detail). New York, Metropolitan Museum.

1197. PIERO DI COSIMO: *The Forest Fire (detail)*. Oxford, Ashmolean Museum.

1198. Piero di Cosimo: *Tondo: Madonna and Child with Angel and Infant S. John.* São Paulo, Museo de Arte.

1199. Piero di Cosimo: *The Discovery of Honey (detail).* Worcester (Mass.), Art Museum.

1200. PIERO DI COSIMO: *Madonna and Child with Infant S. John*. Vaduz, Liechtenstein Collection.

1201. PIERO DI COSIMO: *Immaculate Conception with SS. John Evangelist, Dominic, Catherine, Margaret, Antoninus and Peter.* Florence, Uffizi.

1202. PIERO DI COSIMO: *Story of Prometheus.* Strasbourg, Musée.

1203. Piero di Cosimo: *Madonna and Child with two Angels.*
Venice, Conte Vittorio Cini.

1204. Piero di Cosimo: *Perseus and Andromeda (detail).* Florence, Uffizi.

1205. Copy of the lost *Madonna of the Yarn-Winder*, on which Leonardo was
working in Florence in 1501. Drumlanrig, Duke of Buccleuch.

1206. Leonardo da Vinci: *Mona Lisa*. Paris, Louvre. 1503/05.

1208. Copy of the lost *Leda* on which LEONARDO was working in Florence around 1506. Formerly Paris, Madame de Rublé.

1207. LEONARDO DA VINCI: *Madonna and Child with S. Anne.* Paris, Louvre.

1209. LEONARDO DA VINCI: *Pen Study of Horses for the Battle of Anghiari (1503/05)*. Windsor, Royal Library.
Reproduced by gracious permission of H.M. The Queen.

1210. *Fighting Horsemen in the Battle of Anghiari*. Engraving by L. Zacchia, 1558,
after LEONARDO DA VINCI.

1211. MICHELANGELO: *Black Chalk Study of Nude for the Battle of Cascina* (1504/06). Vienna, Albertina.

1212. Copy of the group known as the *Bathers* in MICHELANGELO's *Battle of Cascina*.
Holkham Hall, Earl of Leicester.

1213. G. TOGNETTI: Drawing of the interior of the Cappella Sistina as it appeared in 1508.

1214. View of the Cappella Sistina as it appears today.

1215. MICHELANGELO: *Fresco: The Deluge (detail)*. Rome, Vatican, Vault of the Cappella Sistina. *1508/12*.

1216, 1217. MICHELANGELO: *Frescoes: An early Sibyl (Delphica) and a late Prophet (Jonah). Rome, Vatican, Vault of the Cappella Sistina. 1508/12.*

1218. MICHELANGELO: *Fresco in corner spandrel near the Last Judgement: Esther and Aman.* Rome, Vatican, Vault of the Cappella Sistina. *1508/12.*

1219. MICHELANGELO: *Fresco in lunette above arched window (right half): Joram.*
Rome, Vatican, Cappella Sistina. *1508/12.*

1220. MICHELANGELO: *Monochrome fresco in medallion: Defeat of the Children of Ahab.*
Rome, Vatican, Vault of the Cappella Sistina. *1508/12.*

1221. MICHELANGELO: *Fresco in spandrel: Josias.* Rome, Vatican, Vault of the Cappella Sistina. *1508/12.*

1222, 1223. MICHELANGELO: *Two marble statues for the Tomb of Pope Julius II:*
The dying Captive—Paris, Louvre (*1514/16*); *The bearded Giant*—Florence, Accademia (*ca 1519*).

1224. PONTORMO on MICHELANGELO's cartoon: *Venus and Cupid*. Florence, Accademia. *1533/34*.

1225. Engraving of MICHELANGELO's lost *Leda* of 1530 (reproduced in reverse).

1226, 1227. MICHELANGELO: *Fresco: Two details of the Last Judgement.* Rome, Vatican, Cappella Sistina. *1534/41.*

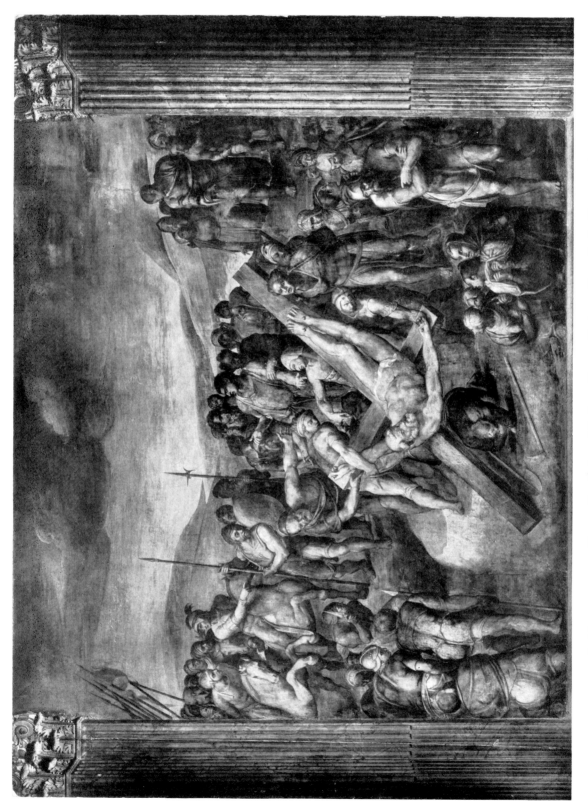

1228. MICHELANGELO: *Fresco: Crucifixion of S. Peter.* Rome, Vatican, Cappella Paolina. 1545/50.

1229. MICHELANGELO: *Cartoon: Holy Family with Infant S. John and other figures.* London, British Museum.

1230. MICHELANGELO: *Pietà* (marble). Florence, S. Maria del Fiore. *Left unfinished in 1556.*

1231. MICHELANGELO's Workshop: *The 'Manchester' Madonna (unfinished)*. London, National Gallery. *ca 1500*.

1232. Early follower of MICHELANGELO: *Tondo: Madonna and Child with Infant S. John.*
Vienna, Akademie.

1233. Early Follower of MICHELANGELO:
Madonna and Child with Infant S. John.
New York, S. H. Kress Foundation.

1234. Early Follower of MICHELANGELO:
Madonna and Child. Homeless.

1235. BACHIACCA: *Lady with music-book.*
Cornbury Park, O. V. Watney.

1235a. BACHIACCA: *Triumph of Time* (*fragment*).
Homeless.

1236. BACHIACCA: *Young Man with lute and, in
background, Triumph of Love.* New Orleans (La.),
Delgado Museum of Art, Kress Collection.

1237. BACHIACCA: *Old Man with skull and, in background,
Triumph of Death.* Cassel, Staatliche Kunstsammlungen.

1238. BACHIACCA: *Version of Michelangelo's Doni Tondo.* Homeless.

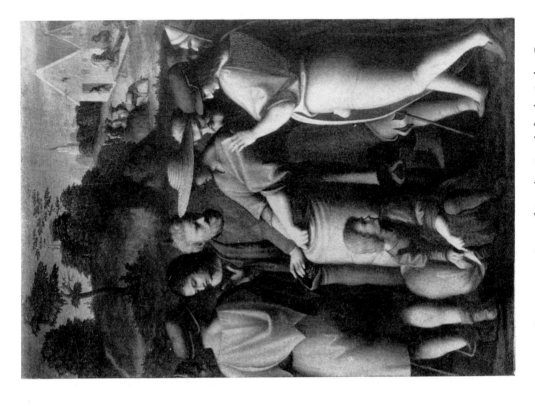

1240. BACHIACCA: *Story of Joseph—Search for the Stolen Cup.* Rome, Galleria Borghese. *ca 1515.*

1239. BACHIACCA: *Madonna and Child with Infant S. John.* Dresden, Gemäldegalerie.

1241. BACHIACCA: *Madonna and Child with S. Elizabeth and Infant S. John.*
Formerly Florence, Serristori Collection.

1242. BACHIACCA: *Holy Family with Infant S. John.*
Formerly Richmond, Cook Collection.

1243. BACHIACCA: *Predella panel: Baptism of S. Acasius (detail)*. Florence, Uffizi. *ca 1521*.

1244. BACHIACCA: *Legend of the Dead King (detail)*. Dresden, Gemäldegalerie. *ca 1523*.

1245. BACHIACCA: *Madonna and Child with Infant S. John*. Homeless.

1246. BACHIACCA: *Tobias and the Angel*.
Formerly Berlin, E. Simon.

1247. BACHIACCA: *Leda*. New York, Jack Linsky.

1248. BACHIACCA: *Beheading of S. John Baptist*. Berlin, Staatliche Museen.

1249. BACHIACCA: *Gathering of Manna* (*detail*). Washington, National Gallery of Art, Kress Collection.

1250. BACHIACCA: *Martyrdom of the Ten Thousand*. Florence, S. Firenze, Cappella del Sacramento.

1251. BACHIACCA: *Tapestry with Grottesche*, after his design. Florence, Gallerie. *1549.*

1252. BACHIACCA: *Tapestry with the Months*, after his design. Florence, Uffizi. *1552/53.*

1253. BUGIARDINI: *Birth of the Baptist*. Stockholm, University. *Signed and dated 1512.*

1254. BUGIARDINI: *The Baptist in the Wilderness.* Formerly London, Lord Northbrook.

1255. BUGIARDINI: *Madonna and Child with Infant S. John.* Nivaagaard, Hage Collection.

1256. Bugiardini: *Portrait of Woman called 'La Monaca'*. Florence, Gallerie Fiorentine.

1257. Bugiardini: *Sleeping Venus*. Venice, Ca'd'Oro.

1259. BUGIARDINI: *Madonna and Child with Infant S. John.* Allentown, Art Museum, Kress Collection. *Signed.*

1258. BUGIARDINI: *Madonna and Child with Infant S. John.* Florence, Gallerie Fiorentine. *Signed and dated 1520.*

1260. BUGIARDINI (and Fra Bartolommeo): *Rape of Dinah.* Vienna, Kunsthistorisches Museum. *1531.*

1261. Bugiardini: *Portrait of Michelangelo*. Florence, Casa Buonarroti.

1262. Bugiardini: *Eve (left half of a Fall of Man)*. Formerly Paris, Lucien Cottreau.

1263. BUGIARDINI: *Martyrdom of S. Catherine*. Florence, S. Maria Novella.

1264. BUGIARDINI: *Madonna adoring the Child with SS. Philip, John Evangelist, Jerome and Joseph.* Berlin, Staatliche Museen. *Signed.*

1265. GRANACCI: *Cassone panel: Annunciation to Zacharias, Visitation, Birth of S. John Baptist.* Formerly Cape Town, Sir Joseph Robinson Collection.

1266. GRANACCI: *Madonna and Child with S. John Baptist and S. Michael.*
Berlin-Ost, Staatliche Museen.

1267. GRANACCI: *Tondo: Madonna and Child.*
New York, Mrs. Borchard.

1268. GRANACCI: *Tondo: Madonna and Child.*
Formerly Ashburnham Place, Lady Ashburnham.

1270 GRANACCI: *Rest on the Flight with Infant S. John.*
Boughton House, Duke of Buccleuch. *Late work.*

1269. GRANACCI: *Rest on the Flight with Infant S. John.*
Dublin, National Gallery of Ireland. *Early work.*

1271. GRANACCI: *Borgherini panel: Joseph with Jacob and his Brothers before Pharaoh. Florence, Uffizi. ca 1515.*

1272. GRANACCI: *Borgherini panel: Joseph taken to prison (detail)*. Florence, Palazzo Davanzati. *ca 1515.*

1273. GRANACCI: *Entry of Charles VIII into Florence*. Florence, Museo Mediceo in Palazzo Riccardi.

1274. GRANACCI: *Madonna and Child with Blessed Gerard of Villamagna and S. Donnino.*
Florence, S. Donnino di Villamagna.

1275. GRANACCI: *Assumption with SS. Bernardo degli Uberti, Fidelis, John Gualbert and Catherine.*
Florence, Accademia.

1276–77. GRANACCI: *Two panels from S. Apollonia: Martyrdom of S. Agatha*—Florence, Accademia; *The Governor of Alexandria commanding the extraction of S. Apollonia's teeth*— Formerly Rossie Priory, Lord Kinnaird.

1278. RIDOLFO GHIRLANDAJO:
Organshutter: S. Cosmas.
Florence, La Quiete.

1279. RIDOLFO GHIRLANDAJO: *Madonna and Child with SS. Francis and Mary Magdalen*
Florence, Accademia. *Dated 1503.*

1280. RIDOLFO GHIRLANDAJO:
Organshutter: S. Damian.
Florence, La Quiete.

1281. RIDOLFO GHIRLANDAJO: *The penitent S. Jerome.* Florence, S. Trinita.

1282. RIDOLFO GHIRLANDAJO: *Way to Calvary*. London, National Gallery.

1283. RIDOLFO GHIRLANDAJO: *Portrait of a Woman.*
Florence, Pitti. *Dated 1509.*

1284. RIDOLFO GHIRLANDAJO: *Portrait of a Man.*
Florence, Marchesa Torrigiani.

1285. RIDOLFO GHIRLANDAJO: *Way to Calvary (detail).* London, National Gallery.

1286. RIDOLFO GHIRLANDAJO: *Portable triptych: Nativity with Benedictine Donor; SS. Benedict, Peter and Ursula; SS. Dorothy, Paul and John Evangelist.* New York, Metropolitan Museum.

1287. RIDOLFO GHIRLANDAJO: *Adoration of the Shepherds with SS. Roch and Sebastian.* Budapest, Museum. *Signed and dated 1510.*

1288. RIDOLFO GHIRLANDAJO: *Frescoes: Trinity and Evangelists.* Florence, Palazzo Vecchio. *ca 1514.*

1289. RIDOLFO GHIRLANDAJO: *Frescoes: Madonna with SS. Benedict and Dominic; Faith and Hope.*
Florence, Colle Ramole, Villa Agostini. *1515/16.*

1290. RIDOLFO GHIRLANDAJO: *S. Zenobius raising a child*. Florence, Accademia. *1517*.

1291. RIDOLFO GHIRLANDAJO: *Altarpiece from S. Pietro Maggiore:*
Madonna and Child with SS. Sebastian, James, John Baptist, Gregory and two female Saints.
Pistoia, Museo Civico. *1528.*

1292. RIDOLFO GHIRLANDAJO: *Lamentation with SS. Jerome, Nicholas and John Baptist.*
Colle Val d'Elsa, S. Agostino. *1521.*

1293. RIDOLFO GHIRLANDAJO: *Cosimo I as a Boy.*
Florence, Museo Mediceo in Palazzo Riccardi. *1531.*

1294. MICHELE DI RIDOLFO: *Lady with Book.*
Florence, Pitti.

1295. MICHELE DI RIDOLFO: *Annunciation with SS. Andrew and Francis (detail).* Fucecchio, Museo.

1296. MICHELE DI RIDOLFO: *Madonna and Child with SS. Michael, Peter, Paul and Mary Magdalen.*
Eastnor Castle, Hon. Mrs. Hervey Bathurst.

1297. MICHELE DI RIDOLFO: *Madonna and Child in Glory with SS. James, Francis, Clare, Lawrence and a donor.*
Florence, Gallerie.

1298. MICHELE DI RIDOLFO: *Leda (detail)*. Rome, Gallerie Borghese.

1299. MICHELE DI RIDOLFO: *La Notte* (after Michelangelo). Roma, Galleria Colonna.

1301. MICHELE DI RIDOLFO: *Madonna and Child with Infant S. John.*
Tynninghame (Prestonkirk, East Lothian), Earl of Haddington.

1300. MICHELE DI RIDOLFO: *Holy Family with Infant S. John.*
Fiesole, Museo Bandini.

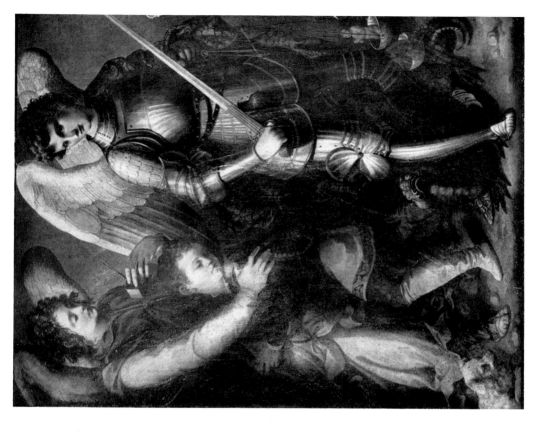

1303. Michele di Ridolfo: *The Archangels (detail)*. Passignano, S. Michele.

1302. Michele di Ridolfo: *Nativity (detail)*. Passignano, S. Michele.

1304. ALBERTINELLI: *Cassone panel: Expulsion from Paradise*. Zagreb, Museum.

1306a. ALBERTINELLI: *Cassone (detail): Creation of Animals and of Man*.
Highnam Court, Gambier Parry Collection.

1305. ALBERTINELLI: *Sacrifice of Isaac.* Formerly London, W. H. Woodward.

1306b. ALBERTINELLI: *Cassone (detail): Creation of Eve and Fall of Man.*
Highnam Court, Gambier Parry Collection.

1307. ALBERTINELLI: *Portable Triptych (open): Madonna and Child, SS. Catherine and Barbara.*
Milan, Museo Poldi Pezzoli. *Dated 1500.*

1308. ALBERTINELLI: *Crucifixion.* Homeless.

1309. ALBERTINELLI: *Madonna and Child.*
Gosford House, Earl of Wemyss and March.

1310. ALBERTINELLI: *Portable Triptych (open). Madonna and Child with SS. Lucy and Apollonia, Angels; God the Father; Annunciation; SS. Michael, Luke, Dominic, Bishop Saint; Crucifixion.* Chartres, Musée.

1311. ALBERTINELLI: *Predella panel: Circumcision.* Florence, Uffizi. *1503.*

1312. ALBERTINELLI: *Visitation*. Florence, Uffizi. *Dated 1503.*

1313. ALBERTINELLI: *Annunciation*. Florence, Accademia. *Signed and dated 1510.*

1315. ALBERTINELLI: *Madonna and Child*. Venice, Seminario.

1314. ALBERTINELLI: *Nativity*. Highnam Court, Gambier Parry Collection.

1317. ALBERTINELLI: *Madonna and Child with Infant S. John. Harewood House, Earl of Harewood. Signed and dated 1509.*

1316. ALBERTINELLI. *Madonna and Child with SS. Jerome and Zenobius. Toulouse, Musée des Augustins. Signed and dated 1506.*

1318. FRA BARTOLOMMEO and ALBERTINELLI: *Fresco: Last Judgement*. Florence, Museo di S. Marco.
1499/1501.

1319. Fra Bartolommeo: *Tondo: Nativity*. Roma, Marchesa Visconti Venosta.

1320. Fra Bartolommeo: *Detail of diptych with Annunciation*. Florence, Gallerie Fiorentine.

1322. FRA BARTOLOMMEO (?): S. Jerome in the Wilderness.
Berlin, Staatliche Museen.

1321. FRA BARTOLOMMEO: Holy Family with Infant S. John.

1323. FRA BARTOLOMMEO: *Vision of S. Bernard*. Florence, Accademia. *1507*.

1324. FRA BARTOLOMMEO: *Madonna and Child with SS. John Baptist, Peter Martyr, Catherine, Mary Magdalen, Benedict and Nicholas* Florence, S. Marco. *Dated 1509.*

1325. FRA BARTOLOMMEO: *Detail of Madonna with SS. Stephen and John Baptist.* Lucca, Duomo. *Signed and dated 1509.*

1326. FRA BARTOLOMMEO: *Holy Family with Infant S. John.*
Firle Place, Lady Gage.

1327. FRA BARTOLOMMEO: *Detail of the Eternal adored by S. Catherine of Siena and the Magdalen.*
Lucca, Pinacoteca. *Dated 1509.*

1328. FRA BARTOLOMMEO: *Madonna in Glory with SS. Sebastian, Stephen, John Baptist, Anthony, Bernard and Cardinal Ferry Carondelet as donor;* in lunette, *Coronation.* The fragments of lunette, Stuttgart, Gemäldegalerie; the rest, Besançon, Cathédrale. *1512.*

1329. FRA BARTOLOMMEO: *Madonna and Child with S. Anne surrounded by Saints.* Florence, Museo di S. Marco. Left unfinished, *1510/15.*

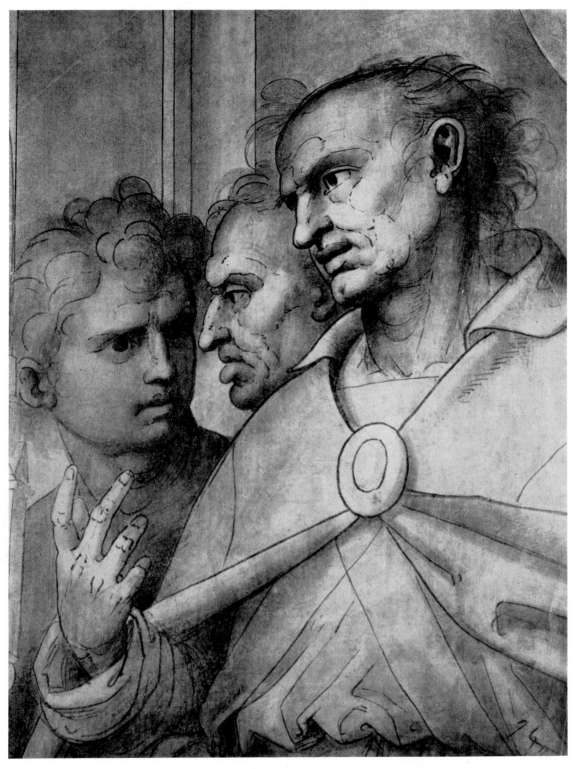

1330. FRA BARTOLOMMEO: *Detail from the unfinished Madonna and Child with S. Anne, surrounded by Saints.*
Florence, Museo di S. Marco. *1510/15.*

1331. FRA BARTOLOMMEO: *Madonna of Humility with music-making Angels.*
Leningrad, Hermitage. *Signed and dated 1515.*

1332. FRA BARTOLOMMEO: *Circumcision.* Vienna, Kunsthistorisches Museum. *1516.*

1333. Fra Paolino: *Annunciation*. Florence, Museo Ferroni.

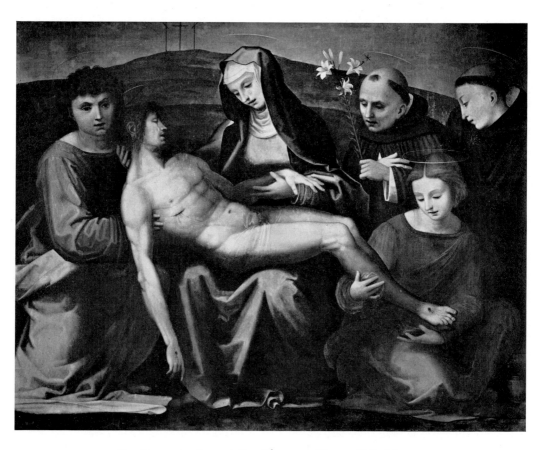

1334. Fra Paolino: *Lamentation*. Florence, Museo di S. Marco. *1519*.

1339. Fra Paolino: *Adoration of the Magi.* Pistoia, S. Domenico. 1526.

1338. Leonardo da Pistoia: *Madonna and Child with SS. Sebastian, Stephen, Laurence and Nicholas. Signed and dated 1516.* Volterra, Pinacoteca.

1341. SOGLIANI on Credi's design: *Madonna adoring the Child with an Angel and Infant S. John*. Palermo, Galleria Nazionale (from Olivella).

1340. LEONARDO DA PISTOIA: *Madonna and Child with goldfinch*. Berlin, Staatliche Museen. *Signed and dated 1516*.

1343. SOGLIANI: *Madonna and Child with Infant S. John.*
Copenhagen, Royal Palace of Amalienborg.

1342. SOGLIANI: *Adoring Angel.* Capesthorne Hall,
Lt. Col. Sir W. H. Davenport.

1344. SOGLIANI: *Christ in the House of Mary and Martha and Donors*. Berlin-Ost, Staatliche Museen.
Dated 1524.

1345. SOGLIANI: *Christ washing the Feet of the Apostles*. Anghiari, Collegiata. *ca 1530*.

1346. SOGLIANI: *Madonna and Child with SS. Bernard and John Baptist.* Florence, Serristori Collection.

1347. Sogliani: *Assumption with SS. Jerome and Anselm*. Empoli, S. Maria a Ripa.

1348. SOGLIANI: *Tobias and the Angel*. Nancy, Musée.

SOGLIANI. Fresco. S. Dominic fed by Angels and Crucifixion with SS. Antonino and Catherine of Siena in background. Florence, Museo di S. Marco. Dated 1536.

1351. Tommaso di Stefano (?): *Madonna nursing the Child and Infant S. John.* Homeless.

1350. Tommaso di Stefano: *Madonna and Infant S. John watching the sleeping Child.* Rome, Galleria Nazionale.

1352–53. TOMMASO DI STEFANO: *Details from 'Capponi' Adoration of the Shepherds (plate 1354).*

1354. TOMMASO DI STEFANO: *Adoration of the Shepherds*. Florence, Villa Capponi ad Arcetri,
Clifford Collection.

1356. TOMMASO DI STEFANO: *Portrait of a Man.* New York,
Metropolitan Museum. *Signed and dated 1521.*

1355. TOMMASO DI STEFANO: *Portrait of a young Man.*
Homeless.

1358. Franciabigio: *Fresco from Villa Dani: Nativity.* Florence, Gallerie Fiorentine. *1510.*

1357. Tommaso di Stefano: *Nativity.* Homeless.

1359. FRANCIABIGIO: *Fresco: Noli me tangere (detail)*. Florence, Museo Horne. *1510.*

1360. FRANCIABIGIO: *Marriage of S. Catherine*.
Rome, Galleria Borghese.

1361. FRANCIABIGIO: *Madonna and Child*. Rome,
Galleria Nazionale. *Signed and dated 1509.*

1362. FRANCIABIGIO: *Fresco: Marriage of the Virgin*. Florence, SS. Annunziata, Atrium. *1513*.

1363. FRANCIABIGIO: *Annunciation*. Turin, Galleria Sabauda.

1364. FRANCIABIGIO: *Madonna with SS. John Baptist and Job*. Florence, Gallerie Fiorentine. *Signed and dated 1516.*

1365. FRANCIABIGIO: *A Jeweller.*
Formerly Brocklesby Park, Earl of Yarborough.
Signed and dated 1516.

1366. FRANCIABIGIO: *A Knight of Rhodes.*
National Gallery, London.
Signed and dated 1514.

1367. FRANCIABIGIO: *The Gardener of Piero
de' Medici.* Hampton Court, Royal Collection.
Signed. Reproduced by gracious permission of H.M. the Queen.

1368. FRANCIABIGIO: *Bust of Man.* Vaduz,
Liechtenstein Collection. *Dated 1517.*

1369. FRANCIABIGIO: *Monochrome fresco: The Meeting of Jesus and the young Baptist in the Wilderness* (*detail*). Florence, Chiostrino dello Scalzo. *1518/19*.

1370. FRANCIABIGIO: *Fresco: Triumph of Cicero*. Florence, Villa di Poggio a Caiano. *1521*.

1371. FRANCIABIGIO: *Portrait of a Man writing*. Berlin, Staatliche Museen. *Signed and dated 1522.*

1372. FRANCIABIGIO: *Madonna and Child with Infant S. John*. Vaduz, Liechtenstein Collection. *Signed*.

1373. FRANCIABIGIO: *Holy Family*. Vienna, Kunsthistorisches Museum.

1374. FRANCIABIGIO: *The Story of Bathsheba* (*detail*). Dresden, Gemäldegalerie. *Signed and dated 1523.*

1375. ANDREA DEL SARTO: *Fresco: Destruction of Bd. Philip Benizzi's Mockers by Lightning.*
Florence, SS. Annunziata, Atrium. *1509/10.*

1376. ANDREA DEL SARTO: *Fresco: Arrival of the Magi.* Florence, SS. Annunziata, Atrium. *Signed. 1511.*

1378. ANDREA DEL SARTO: *Monochrome fresco: Charity.* Florence, Chiostrino dello Scalzo. *1512/15.*

1377. ANDREA DEL SARTO: *Annunciation from San Gallo.* Florence, Pitti. *Signed.*

1380. Sixteenth-century version of ANDREA DEL SARTO's lost fresco in the Tabernacolo di Porta a Pinti.

1379. ANDREA DEL SARTO: *Marriage of S. Catherine with S. Margaret and Infant S. John.* Dresden, Gemäldegalerie. *Signed.*

1381. ANDREA DEL SARTO: *Fresco: Birth of the Virgin (detail)*. Florence, SS. Annunziata, Atrium.
Signed and dated 1514.

1382. ANDREA DEL SARTO: *Early Self-portrait.*
Florence, Uffizi.

1383. ANDREA DEL SARTO: *The artist's Wife (?).*
Madrid, Prado.

1384. ANDREA DEL SARTO: *A French Lady.*
Cleveland, Museum of Art. *1518/19.*

1385. ANDREA DEL SARTO: *A young Man.*
Philadelphia, Johnson Collection.

1386. Andrea del Sarto: *Charity*. Paris, Louvre. *Signed and dated 1518.*

1387. ANDREA DEL SARTO: *Madonna and Child with SS. Elizabeth, Catherine and Infant S. John*, painted for the King of France. Leningrad, Hermitage. *Signed. 1519.*

1388–1389. ANDREA DEL SARTO: *Monochrome frescoes: Baptism of the People* (1517); *Beheading of S. John Baptist* (1523). Florence, Chiostrino dello Scalzo.

1390. ANDREA DEL SARTO: '*La Madonna della Scala*'. Madrid, Prado.

1391. ANDREA DEL SARTO: *The 'Passerini' Assumption, with SS. Nicholas and Margaret of Cortona.*
Florence, Pitti, *ca 1526.*

1392. ANDREA DEL SARTO: *Madonna and Child with SS. Bruno, Peter, Onuphrius, Celsus, Julia, Catherine, Mark and Anthony of Padua; Annunciation.* Berlin, Staatliche Museen (the lunette—Florence, Pitti). *Dated 1528.*

1393. ANDREA DEL SARTO: *Fresco on tile: Late Self-portrait*. Florence, Uffizi.

1394. ANDREA DEL SARTO: *Unfinished portrait of a Woman*. Windsor Castle, Royal Collection.

Reproduced by gracious permission of H.M. the Queen.

1395. ANDREA DEL SARTO: *Predella panel from the Vallombrosa altarpiece: S. Michael and Lucifer fighting for a Soul*. Florence, Uffizi. *1528*.

1396. ANDREA DEL SARTO: *Sacrifice of Isaac*. Dresden, Gemäldegalerie. *Signed*.

1397. PULIGO: *Madonna of Humility with Infant S. John in background*. Montpellier, Musée.

1398. PULIGO: *Madonna of Humility with Infant S. John in background*. Rome, Galleria Borghese.

1399. PULIGO: *Madonna and Child with Infant S. John*. Formerly Naples, Duca di Montaltino.

1400. PULIGO: *Madonna and Child with (?) Infant S. John*. Roma, Museo di Palazzo Venezia.

1401. PULIGO: *Vision of S. Bernard*. Baltimore, Walters Art Gallery.

1402. PULIGO: *Portrait of a Woman*. Florence, Museo di S. Salvi.

1403. PULIGO: *Portrait of a young Monsignore*. Oakly Park, Earl of Plymouth.

1404. PULIGO: *Early portrait of Carnesecchi*.
Bowood, Marquess of Lansdowne.

1405. PULIGO: *Portrait of a Man*.
Berlin, Staatliche Museen.

1406. PULIGO: *Later portrait of Carnesecchi*.
Florence, Pitti.

1407. PULIGO: *'Il Fattore di S. Marco'*.
Firle Place, Lady Gage.

1408. PULIGO: *Madonna and blessing Child* (destroyed). Vienna, Akademie.

1409. PULIGO: *Madonna and Child with two Angels*. Formerly London, Saunders Collection.

1410. PULIGO: *Lucretia*. Cincinnati (Ohio),
I. Signer Collection.

1411. PULIGO: *Cleopatra*. Formerly Budapest,
Lederer Collection.

1412. PULIGO: *S. Barbara*. Leningrad, Hermitage.

1413. PULIGO: *A female Martyr*. Homeless.

1414. PULIGO: *A Lady with a music book*. Salisbury, Julian Salmond.

1415. PULIGO: *Madonna and Child surrounded by six Saints (detail)*.
Florence, S. Maria Maddalena de'Pazzi.

1416. PULIGO: *Madonna and Child worshipped by SS. Quentin and Placidus*.
Sarasota, Ringling Museum.

1417. PONTORMO: *Fresco: S. Veronica.* Florence, S. Maria Novella, Cappella del Papa. *1515.*

1418. PONTORMO: *Fresco from S. Ruffillo: Madonna and Child with SS. Lucy, Agnes(?),*
Zacharias and Michael. Florence, SS. Annunziata, Cappella di S. Luca.

1419. PONTORMO: *Fresco: Visitation*. Florence, SS. Annunziata, Atrium. *1516*.

1420. PONTORMO: *Borgherini panel: Joseph sold to Potiphar*. Grey Walls, Lady Salmond. *After 1515.*

1421. Pontormo: *Holy Family with SS. John Evangelist, Francis, James, and Infant S. John.*
Florence, S. Michele Visdomini. *Dated 1518.*

1422. PONTORMO: *A Discussion*. London, National Gallery.

1423. PONTORMO: *Madonna and Child with SS. Jerome and Francis and two Angels.* Florence, Uffizi.

1425. PONTORMO: *Two young Men with a letter.* Venice, Conte Vittorio Cini.

1424. PONTORMO: *Madonna and Child with Infant S. John.* Florence, Galleria Corsini.

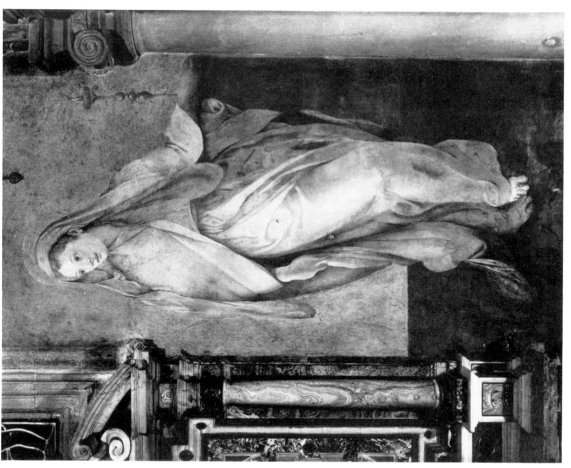

1426. Pontormo: *Fresco: Annunciation.* Florence, S. Felicita. *1526/28.*

1427. PONTORMO: *Fresco: Christ before Pilate.* Florence, Certosa del Galluzzo. *1522/27.*

1428. PONTORMO: *Visitation*. Florence, Pieve di Carmignano.

1429. PONTORMO: *Decimation of the Theban Legion (detail)*. Florence, Pitti.

1430. PONTORMO: *A young Halberdier.*
New York, C. D. Stillman.

1431. PONTORMO: *Maria Salviati with young Cosimo I.*
Baltimore, Walters Art Gallery.

1432. PONTORMO: *A young Medici* (?).
Lucca, Pinacoteca.

1433. PONTORMO: *Alessandro de'Medici called
il Moro.* Philadelphia, Johnson Collection. *ca 1535.*

1434. PONTORMO: *Noli me tangere*, on Michelangelo's cartoon. Homeless. *1531*.

1435. PONTORMO: *Pygmalion and Galatea*. Rome, Delegazione per le Restituzioni (formerly Principe Barberini).

1436. PONTORMO: *Chiaroscuro: Jacob and Rebecca deceiving old Isaac*. Florence, Uffizi.

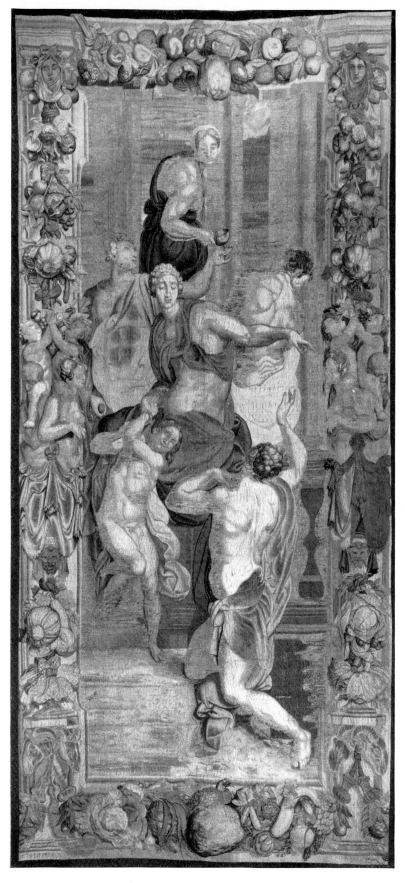

1437. Tapestry on PONTORMO's design: *Benjamin detained at Pharaoh's court.*
Rome, Palazzo del Quirinale. *1549.*

1438. Tapestry on PONTORMO's design: *Jacob's Lament*. Rome, Palazzo del Quirinale. *1553.*

1439. BRONZINO: *Fresco: S. Benedict in the Wilderness*. Florence, Badia, Cloister. *ca 1523*.

1440. BRONZINO: *Madonna and Child with Infant S. John*. Homeless.

1441. BRONZINO: *Adoration of the Shepherds*. Budapest, Museum. *Signed*.

1443. Bronzino: *Maria Salviati(?)*. San Francisco (Cal.),
De Young Memorial Museum, Kress Collection.

1442. Bronzino: *Bartolomeo Panciatichi*. Florence, Uffizi.

1445. BRONZINO: *Cosimo de' Medici*. Toledo (Ohio), Museum of Art.

1444. BRONZINO: *Cosimo de' Medici(?) as Orpheus*. Philadelphia (Pa.), Museum of Art.

1446. BRONZINO: *Eleonora da Toledo, wife of Cosimo I, and her son Ferdinando.* Cincinnati (Ohio),
Art Museum.

1447. BRONZINO: *The 'Panciatichi' Holy Family with Infant S. John*. Florence, Uffizi.

1448. Bronzino: *Pietà*. Besançon, Musée. *Signed. 1545*.

1449. BRONZINO: *Don Garzia de'Medici as a child*. Florence, Uffizi.

1450. BRONZINO: *Don Garzia (?) de'Medici as a boy*. Oxford, Ashmolean Museum.

1451. BRONZINO: *Admiral Andrea Doria as Neptune*. Milan, Brera.

1452. BRONZINO: *Stefano Colonna in armour*. Rome, Galleria Nazionale. *Signed and dated 1546*.

1453. BRONZINO: *Venus, Cupid and Jealousy*. Budapest, Museum.

1454. Bronzino: *Fresco: Crossing of the Red Sea.* Florence, Palazzo Vecchio, Cappella di Eleonora. 1541/42.

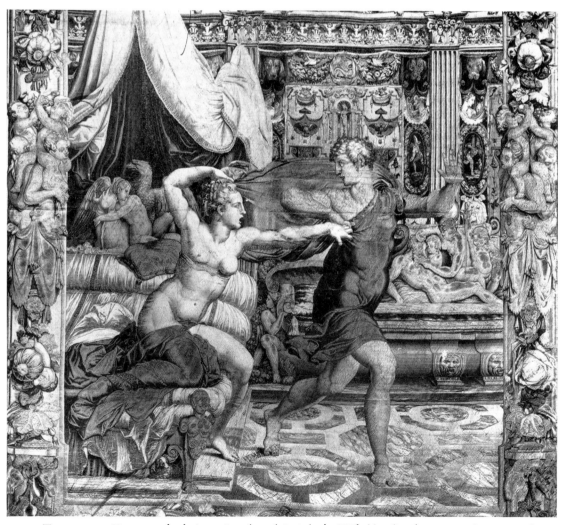

1455. Tapestry on Bronzino's design: *Joseph and Potiphar's Wife (detail).* Florence, Palazzo Vecchio, Sala dei Dugento. *Signed.* 1549.

1456. Bronzino: *Fresco: The Brazen Serpent (detail)*. Florence, Palazzo Vecchio, Cappella di Eleonora. *1542*.

1457. Bronzino: *Descent into Limbo* (detail). Florence, Opera di S. Croce. *Signed and dated 1552.*

1458. BRONZINO and Assistants: *The Raising of the daughter of Jairus (detail)*. Florence, S. Maria Novella.

1460. BRONZINO: *The Poetess Laura Battiferri Ammannati.*
Florence, Palazzo Vecchio, Loeser Bequest.

1459. BRONZINO: *Eleonora da Toledo in middle age.* Washington,
National Gallery of Art, Kress Collection. *ca 1560.*

1461. ROSSO: *Madonna and Child with four Saints* (from S. Maria Nuova). Florence, Uffizi. 1517.

1462. ROSSO: *Madonna and Child with S. Anne, Infant S. John and Angels.* Los Angeles (Cal.), County Museum.

1464. ROSSO: *Young Man sitting on a table.* Naples, Capodimonte. *ca 1523.*

1463. ROSSO: *Young Man with helmet.* Liverpool, Walker Art Gallery. *Signed.*

1465. ROSSO: *Deposition*. Volterra, Pinacoteca. *Signed and dated 1521*.

1466. ROSSO: *Marriage of the Virgin*. Florence, S. Lorenzo. *Signed and dated 1523.*

1468. ROSSO: *Detail from Moses defending the Daughters of Jethro.*
Florence, Uffizi. 1523.

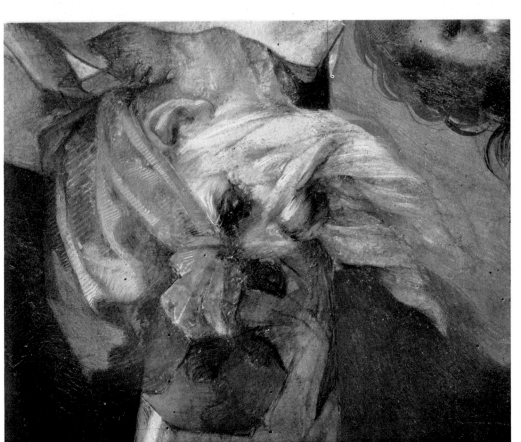

1467. ROSSO: *Detail from the Deposition* (Plate 1465).
Volterra, Pinacoteca. 1521.

1470. ROSSO: *The dead Christ supported by four Angels.* Boston, Museum of Fine Arts. *Signed.* 1524/27.

1469. ROSSO: *Madonna and Child in Glory.* Leningrad, Hermitage.

1471. Rosso: *Transfiguration*. Città di Castello, Duomo. *1528/30*.

1472. ROSSO: *Deposition (detail)*. Borgo San Sepolcro, Orfanelle. *1528.*

1473. ROSSO: *Pietà*. Paris, Louvre. *1537/40.*

1474. ROSSO: *Fresco: The Fountain of Youth.* Fontainebleau, Galerie François I. 1534/37.

1475. ROSSO: *Fresco: The Death of Adonis.* Fontainebleau, Galerie François I. 1534/37.

1476. Rosso: *Fresco and stucco decoration: The Burning of Catania.* Fontainebleau, Galerie François I. 1534/37.

1477. Tapestry after one of Rosso's decorations at Fontainebleau: *The Unity of the State*. Vienna, Kunsthistorisches Museum.

1478. Sellajo: *View of Florence*. Detail from Plate 1109.

TOPOGRAPHICAL INDEX

Baltimore. As the numbers of all paintings in the Walters Art Gallery are preceded by the number 37, this prefix has been omitted.

Florence, GALLERIE. Pictures which are not currently exhibited are listed under this general heading.

A few pictures in Florence have an inventory number followed by 'Dep'; this does not imply that they are stored in the 'depositi' or not exhibited.

Paris, MUSÉES NATIONAUX. Pictures from the Campana Collection, which were distributed among various French provincial museums, have been listed under Paris, in view of the plan to unite all early Italian pictures from the Campana Collection.

Richmond (Surrey). For the sake of convenient reference, pictures in the Cook Collection have been listed under their old location. The collection has, in fact, been split up and many paintings are on temporary loan to various museums in Britain.

TOPOGRAPHICAL INDEX

3

Arezzo (*contd.*) S. FRANCESCO: Bicci di Lorenzo, Master of the Arte della Lana Coronation, Neri di Bicci, Paolo Schiavo, Spinello Aretino.

S. MARIA DELLA PIEVE: Spinello Aretino.

S. MARIA MADDALENA: Spinello Aretino.

S. MICHELE: Neri di Bicci.

CONSERVATORIO DI S. CATERINA: Parri Spinelli.

OSPEDALE: Jacopo del Casentino.

(Environs). S. MARIA DELLE GRAZIE: Bicci di Lorenzo, Parri Spinelli.

Argiano (San Casciano, Val di Pesa). S. MARIA E ANGIOLO: Unidentified Florentine 1420–1465.

Arles. MUSÉE RÉATTU: Giusto d'Andrea.

Arundel Castle (Sussex). DUKE OF NORFOLK (EX): Master of S. Miniato.

Ascott (Bucks.). NATIONAL TRUST: Andrea del Sarto.

Ashburnham Place (Sussex). LADY ASHBURNHAM (EX): Botticini, Giovanni dal Ponte, Granacci.

Assisi. S. CHIARA: Maso di Banco.

S. FRANCESCO, LOWER CHURCH: Cimabue, Giotto, Giotto Assistants, Giotto Followers, Maso di Banco.

— UPPER CHURCH: Cimabue, Giotto, Master of S. Cecilia.

— TREASURY: Pollajuolo.

S. RUFINUCCIO: Maso di Banco.

EDUCATORIO DI S. GIUSEPPE: Maso di Banco.

MRS. F. M. PERKINS: Francesco di Antonio, Lorenzo Monaco, Lorenzo di Niccolò, Mariotto di Nardo, Master of the Bambino Vispo, Master of S. Miniato, Niccolò di Tommaso, Pier Francesco Fiorentino, Piero di Cosimo, Unidentified Florentine 1350–1420.

Athens. BENAKIS MUSEUM: Sellajo.

Athens (Georgia). UNIVERSITY OF GEORGIA: Fra Diamante, Paolo Schiavo.

Atlanta (Georgia): ART ASSOCIATION GALLERIES: Bartolomeo di Giovanni.

Autun. MUSÉE ROLIN: Botticini.

Auxerre. MUSÉE DES BEAUX-ARTS: Niccolò di Tommaso.

Avignon. MUSÉE CALVET: Machiavelli, Mariotto di Nardo, Niccolò di Pietro Gerini, Unidentified Florentine 1420–1465.

Badia a Rusti (Chianti). S. PIETRO: Neri di Bicci.

Bagnères-de-Bigorre. MUSÉE SALLES: Unidentified Florentine 1420–1465.

Bagno di Romagna. S. MARIA DEL FIORE: Mainardi, Neri di Bicci.

Balcarres (Fife). EARL OF CRAWFORD AND BALCARRES: Apollonio di Giovanni, Bicci di Lorenzo (EX), Botticelli, Botticini, Bugiardini (EX), Filippino Lippi, Filippo Lippi, Mainardi, Mariotto di Nardo, Pseudo Pier Francesco Fiorentino, Sellajo, 'Tommaso' (EX), Unidentified Florentine 1350–1420, Unidentified Florentine 1420–1465.

Balmville (Newburgh, N.Y.). MISS TESSIE JONES: Benedetto Ghirlandajo, Nardo di Cione.

Baltimore. WALTERS ART GALLERY: Andrea di Giusto, Bartolomeo di Giovanni, Bicci di Lorenzo, Daddi, Francesco di Antonio, Giovanni del Biondo, Granacci, Filippo Lippi, Lorenzo Monaco, Machiavelli, Mariotto di Nardo, Master of the Bambino Vispo, Master of the Castello Nativity, Neri di Bicci, Niccolò di Tommaso, Pseudo Pier Francesco Fiorentino, Pontormo, Puligo, Raffaellino del Garbo, Rosselli, Rossello di Jacopo, Sellajo, Sogliani, 'Tommaso', 'Utili', Unidentified Florentine 1350–1420,

Unidentified Florentine 1465–1540.

MUSEUM OF ART: Bachiacca, Botticelli, Botticini, Lorenzo Monaco, Niccolò di Pietro Gerini, 'Utili'.

DR. GEORGE REULING (EX): Rosso Fiorentino, Unidentified Florentine 1465–1540.

Banbury, see Upton House.

Barberino di Mugello. COMPAGNIA DEI SS. SEBASTINO E ROCCO: Puligo.

(Environs). BADIA DI VIGESIMO: Rosselli.

— COLLE BARUCCI, S. MARIA: Neri di Bicci.

Barcelona. MUSEO DE ARTE DE CATALUÑA: Francesco di Antonio, Master of the Lathrop Tondo, Neri di Bicci, Rossello di Jacopo.

DONA HELENA CAMBÒ DE GUARDANS: Botticelli.

Bari. PINACOTECA PROVINCIALE: Puligo.

Barnard Castle (Durham). BOWES MUSEUM: Franciabigio, Mainardi.

Bassano. MUSEO CIVICO: 'Tommaso'.

Bayonne. MUSÉE BONNAT: Botticelli, Daddi, Davide Ghirlandajo, Jacopo di Cione, Pier Francesco Fiorentino, 'Utili'.

Beaumesnil. M. FURSTEMBERGER: Piero di Cosimo.

Belgrade. ROYAL PALACE (EX): 'Utili'.

Belton House (Grantham, Lincs.). EARL BROWNLOW: Fra Bartolommeo.

Berchtesgaden. SCHLOSS: Bartolomeo di Giovanni.

Berea (Kentucky). COLLEGE: Cristiani, Pesellino, Raffaellino del Garbo, Unidentified Florentine 1350–1420.

Bergamo. ACCADEMIA CARRARA: Albertinelli, Bachiacca, Baldovinetti, Bartolomeo di Giovanni, Botticelli, Botticini, Bronzino, Domenico di Michelino, Ridolfo Ghirlandajo, Lorenzo Monaco, Machiavelli, Mariotto di Nardo, Michele di Ridolfo, Pesellino, Pseudo Pier Francesco Fiorentino, Pontormo, Sellajo, 'Tommaso'.

Bergen. MUSEUM: Bugiardini.

Berkeley (Cal.). EPISCOPAL STUDENT CENTER: Andrea da Firenze.

Berlin. EHEMALS STAATLICHE MUSEEN (DAHLEM): Albertinelli, Andrea di Giusto, Andrea del Sarto, Fra Angelico, Bachiacca, Fra Bartolommeo, Bicci di Lorenzo, Botticelli, Botticini, Bronzino, Bugiardini, Castagno, Daddi, Domenico di Michelino, Domenico Veneziano, Franciabigio, Agnolo Gaddi, Taddeo Gaddi, Davide Ghirlandajo, Domenico Ghirlandajo, Ridolfo Ghirlandajo, Giotto, Giotto Assistant, Giovanni di Francesco, Giusto d'Andrea, Gozzoli, Granacci, Jacopo del Casentino, Jacopo di Cione, Leonardo da Pistoia, Filippino Lippi, Filippo Lippi, Lorenzo di Credi, Lorenzo Monaco, Lorenzo di Niccolò, Machiavelli, Mainardi, Mariotto di Nardo, Masaccio, Maso di Banco, Master of the Bambino Vispo, Michele di Ridolfo, Niccolò di Pietro Gerini, Paolo Schiavo, Pesellino, Pseudo Pier Francesco Fiorentino, Piero di Cosimo, Pollajuolo, Pontormo, Puligo, Raffaellino del Garbo, Rosselli, Rossello di Jacopo, Sellajo, 'Utili', Verrocchio, Unidentified Florentine 1350–1420, Unidentified Florentine 1465–1540.

— PRINT ROOM: Botticelli, Lorenzo Monaco.

BERLIN-OST: Bachiacca, Fra Bartolommeo, Bugiardini, Agnolo Gaddi, Davide Ghirlandajo, Granacci, Filippino Lippi, Lorenzo di Credi, Mainardi, Master of the Bambino Vispo, Neri di Bicci, Paolo Schiavo, Rosselli, Rosso Fiorentino, Sellajo, Sogliani, 'Tommaso'.

6

Berlin (*contd.*) KUNSTGEWERBEMUSEUM: Bugiardini.

DR. PAUL BONN: Raffaellino del Garbo.

HERR BRACHT (EX): Pesellino.

VON BECKERATH (EX): Andrea da Firenze.

VON GOLDAMMER (EX): Daddi.

KAUFMANN COLLECTION (EX): Raffaellino del Garbo.

RICHARD VON KAUFMANN (EX): Mariotto di Nardo.

GRAF SAURMA (EX): Bugiardini.

EUGEN SCHWEITZER (EX): Franciabigio.

EDUARD SIMON (EX): Bachiacca.

W. WEISBACH (EX): Giovanni di Francesco.

Bernay. MUSÉE MUNICIPAL: Taddeo Gaddi.

Berne. KUNSTMUSEUM: Fra Angelico, Daddi, Taddeo Gaddi, Jacopo del Casentino, Masolino, Nardo di Cione.

Besançon. MUSÉE DES BEAUX-ARTS: Botticelli, Bronzino, Machiavelli, Niccolò di Tommaso, 'Utili'.

CATHEDRAL: Fra Bartolommeo.

Beverley Hills (Cal.). MISS MARION DAVIES (EX): Raffaellino del Garbo.

Béziers. MUSÉE DES BEAUX-ARTS: Gozzoli.

Bibbiena (Casentino): PROPOSITURA (S. IPPOLITO): Bicci di Lorenzo.

(Environs). S. MARIA DEL SASSO: Bicci di Lorenzo, Fra Paolino.

Biella. ORESTE RIVETTI: Cristiani.

Bignor Park (Pulborough, Sussex). VISCOUNTESS MERSEY: Bronzino.

Bilbao. LAUREANO JADO: Bartolomeo di Giovanni.

Birmingham. BARBER INSTITUTE: Andrea del Sarto, Botticelli.

CITY ART GALLERY: Botticelli.

Birmingham (Alabama). MUSEUM OF ART: Apollonio di Giovanni, Francesco di Antonio, Franciabigio, Agnolo Gaddi, Mainardi, Mariotto di Nardo, Niccolò di Pietro Gerini, Pesellino, Rosselli, Sellajo, 'Utili'.

Blaricum (Holland). DR. J. P. KLEIWEG DE ZWAAN: Mariotto di Nardo.

Bloomington (Ind.). UNIVERSITY OF INDIANA: Taddeo Gaddi, Unidentified Florentine 1420–1465.

Bologna. PINACOTECA: Bugiardini, Franciabigio, Giotto Assistant, Lorenzo Monaco, Master of S. Miniato.

S. DOMENICO: Filippino Lippi, Michelangelo.

S. MARIA DEI SERVI: Cimabue.

Bonn. PROVINZIALMUSEUM: Bartolomeo di Giovanni, Bugiardini, Mainardi, Master of the Bambino Vispo.

Bordeaux. MUSÉE DES BEAUX-ARTS: Giovanni da Milano, Jacopo del Casentino, Master of the Bambino Vispo, Sellajo.

PIERRE CHAPANNAN (EX): Pontormo.

Borgo alla Collina (Casentino). S. DONATO: Master of the Bambino Vispo.

Borgo San Lorenzo (Mugello). S. LORENZO: Niccolò di Pietro Gerini, Rossello di Jacopo.

ORATORIO DEL CROCIFISSO DEI MIRACOLI (EX): Piero di Cosimo.

Borgo San Sepolcro. PINACOTECA COMUNALE: Pontormo.

ORFANELLE: Rosso Fiorentino.

Borselli (Pontassieve). S. MARGHERITA DI TOSINA: Mariotto di Nardo.

Boston (Mass.). MUSEUM OF FINE ARTS: Andrea di Giusto, Fra Angelico, Antonio Veneziano, Bicci di Lorenzo, Botticelli, Bronzino, Daddi, Granacci, Jacopo del Casentino, Leonardo da Pistoia, Machiavelli, Mainardi, Master of the Bambino Vispo, Master of the Barberini Panels, Master of S. Miniato, Niccolò di Pietro Gerini, Niccolò di Tommaso, Rosselli, Rosso Fiorentino, Sellajo.

    ISABELLA STEWART GARDNER MUSEUM: Alunno di Benozzo, Fra Angelico, Bachiacca, Bicci di Lorenzo, Botticelli, Botticini, Bronzino, Daddi, Domenico Veneziano, Giotto Assistant, Giovanni di Francesco, Jacopo di Cione, Lorenzo di Credi, Masaccio, Niccolò di Pietro Gerini, Pesellino, Pollajuolo.

    ROBERT J. EDWARDS (EX): Giusto d'Andrea.

    QUINCEY SHAW (EX): Botticini.

Boughton House (Northants.). DUKE OF BUCCLEUCH: Granacci, Puligo.

Bourges. MUSÉE DU BERRY: Francesco di Antonio, Niccolò di Pietro Gerini.

Boville Ernica (Frosinone). S. PIETRO ISPANO: Giotto.

Bowood (Calne, Wilts.). MARQUESS OF LANSDOWNE: Puligo.

Brandenburg. WREDOWSCHE ZEICHENSCHULE: Sellajo.

Brant Broughton (Lincs.). REV. CANON SUTTON (EX): Mariotto di Nardo.

Bremen. KUNSTHALLE: Bachiacca, Jacopo del Casentino, Masolino, 'Utili'.

Breslau. SCHLESISCHES MUSEUM: Leonardo da Pistoia, Rosselli, Sellajo.

Bristol. CITY ART GALLERY: Jacopo del Casentino.

Brocklesby Park (Lincs.). EARL OF YARBOROUGH: Bachiacca, Franciabigio (EX).

Brolio (Chianti). BARONE RICASOLI: Taddeo Gaddi, Lorenzo di Niccolò.

Brooklyn (N.Y.). BROOKLYN MUSEUM: Lorenzo Monaco, Lorenzo di Niccolò, Mainardi, Maso di Banco, Neri di Bicci, Pseudo Pier Francesco Fiorentino, Sellajo.

    MICHAEL FRIEDSAM (EX): Fra Angelico.

Bruges. NOTRE-DAME: Michelangelo.

Brunswick. HERZOG ANTON ULRICH MUSEUM: Alvaro Portoghese, Bicci di Lorenzo, Lorenzo di Credi, Mariotto di Nardo, Niccolò di Pietro Gerini.

Brunswick (Maine). BOWDOIN COLLEGE: Unidentified Florentine 1420–1465, Unidentified Florentine 1465–1540.

Brussels. MUSÉES ROYAUX DES BEAUX-ARTS: Franciabigio, Giovanni dal Ponte, Jacopo del Casentino, Leonardo da Pistoia, Fra Paolino, Puligo, Sogliani.

    VAN GELDER: Daddi.

    MME. PAUL PECHÈRE: Daddi.

    MME. FERON-STOCLET: Giotto Follower, Lorenzo Monaco, Unidentified Florentine 1350–1420.

    JACQUES STOCLET: Master of S. Cecilia.

    MLLE. MICHÈLE STOCLET: Daddi, Niccolò di Tommaso.

    PHILIPPE STOCLET: Pseudo Pier Francesco Fiorentino.

Bucharest. MUSEUM: Domenico Veneziano.

Budapest. MUSEUM OF FINE ARTS: Andrea del Sarto, Bachiacca, Bronzino, Fra Diamante, Francesco di Antonio, Ridolfo Ghirlandajo, Giovanni dal Ponte, Granacci, Jacopo del Casentino, Jacopo di Cione, Filippino Lippi, Lorenzo Monaco, Mainardi, Mariotto di Nardo, Maso di Banco, Master of S. Cecilia, Neri di Bicci, Pseudo Pier Francesco Fiorentino, Puligo, Raffaellino del Garbo, Sellajo, Spinello Aretino, 'Utili'.

Budapest (*contd.*) FRIEDRICH GLÜCK (EX): Master of S. Miniato.
    LEDERER COLLECTION (EX): Puligo.
    SIMON MELLER: Mariotto di Nardo.
Buenos Aires. MRS. M. R. VON BUCH: Sellajo.
    PELLERANO COLLECTION: Master of S. Miniato.
Buffalo (N.Y.). ALBRIGHT ART GALLERY: Giovanni del Biondo, Rossello di Jacopo, 'Tommaso'.
Buscot Park (Faringdon, Berks.). LORD FARINGDON: Botticelli.

Caen. MUSÉE DES BEAUX-ARTS: Sellajo.
Calenzano (Prato). S. NICCOLÒ: Jacopo di Cione.
Cambiano (Val d'Elsa). S. PROSPERO: Jacopo del Casentino.
Cambridge. FITZWILLIAM MUSEUM: Albertinelli, Apollonio di Giovanni, Bartolomeo di
    Giovanni, Botticini, Domenico Veneziano, Francesco di Antonio, Davide Ghir-
    landajo, Giovanni dal Ponte, Filippo Lippi, Lorenzo Monaco, Mainardi, Mariotto di
    Nardo, Master of the Castello Nativity, Niccolò di Pietro Gerini, Rosselli, Rossello di
    Jacopo, Sellajo, 'Tommaso'.
Cambridge (Mass.). FOGG ART MUSEUM: Albertinelli, Andrea di Giusto, Fra Angelico, Bicci
    di Lorenzo, Botticelli, Daddi, Giovanni del Biondo, Giovanni dal Ponte, Gozzoli,
    Jacopo di Cione, Filippino Lippi, Filippo Lippi, Lorenzo di Credi, Mariotto di Nardo,
    Master of the Bambino Vispo, Master of the Castello Nativity, Neri di Bicci, Pesel-
    lino, Pseudo Pier Francesco Fiorentino, Piero di Cosimo, Raffaellino del Garbo,
    Sellajo, Spinello Aretino, 'Utili', Unidentified Florentine 1350–1420.
    RADCLIFFE COLLEGE: Mainardi.
    EDWARD FORBES: Domenico Ghirlandajo.
    SIDNEY J. FREEDBERG: Piero di Cosimo.
    MRS. A. KINGSLEY PORTER: Niccolò di Pietro Gerini, Unidentified Florentine 1420–1465.
Campi Bisenzio (Firenze). PIEVE: Unidentified Florentine 1465–1540.
Cannes. FRANK GOULD: Taddeo Gaddi.
Canneto (Val d'Elsa). S. GIORGIO: Neri di Bicci.
Capesthorne Hall (Macclesfield). LT. COL. SIR W. H. BROMLEY DAVENPORT: Giotto Follower,
    Master of S. Miniato, Niccolò di Pietro Gerini, Sogliani, Spinello Aretino.
Cape Town. SIR JOSEPH ROBINSON (EX): Bartolomeo di Giovanni, Domenico di Michelino,
    Granacci, Piero di Cosimo.
Cappiano (Valdarno Superiore). S. LORENZO: Raffaellino del Garbo.
Carcassonne. MUSÉE DES BEAUX-ARTS: Francesco di Antonio.
Carrara. ACCADEMIA: Botticini.
Casalguidi (Pistoia). S. PIERO: Leonardo da Pistoia.
Cassel. GEMÄLDEGALERIE: Bachiacca, Bartolomeo di Giovanni, Fra Diamante.
Castelfiorentino (Val d'Elsa). S. VERDIANA (PINACOTECA PARROCCHIALE): Taddeo Gaddi,
    Granacci.
    CAPPELLA DELLA VISITAZIONE: Gozzoli.
    (Environs). S. MARIA LUNGO TUONO: Rosselli.
Castell'Arquato (Piacenza). MUSEO PARROCCHIALE: Pseudo Pier Francesco Fiorentino.
Castelnuovo (Val d'Elsa): S. BARBARA: Pier Francesco Fiorentino.
    S. MARIA ASSUNTA: Neri di Bicci.
    ORATORIO DELLA MADONNA DELLA TOSSE: Gozzoli.

Castelnuovo Garfagnana. DUOMO: Sogliani.

Castiglion Fiorentino (Val di Chiana). PINACOTECA: Taddeo Gaddi, Pseudo Pier Francesco Fiorentino, Sellajo, 'Tommaso'.
  COLLEGIATA: Lorenzo di Credi, Sogliani.

Castiglion d'Olona. BATTISTERO: Masolino.
  COLLEGIATA: Masolino, Neri di Bicci, Paolo Schiavo.
  PALAZZO CASTIGLIONE: Masolino.

Castle Ashby (Northants.). MARQUESS OF NORTHAMPTON: Botticini.

Certaldo. PALAZZO DEI PRIORI: Giusto d'Andrea, Pier Francesco Fiorentino.
  CAPPELLA DEL PONTE DELL'AGLIENA: Gozzoli, Pier Francesco Fiorentino.

Certomondo (Casentino). S. MARIA ASSUNTA: Neri di Bicci.

Cetica (Casentino). S. ANGELO: Pesellino.
  S. MARIA: Bicci di Lorenzo.

Châalis (Ermenonville). MUSÉE JACQUEMART-ANDRÉ: Giotto.

Chambéry. MUSÉE DES BEAUX-ARTS: Alunno di Benozzo, Cimabue, Domenico di Michelino, Masaccio, Fra Paolino.

Chantilly. MUSÉE CONDÉ: Fra Angelico, Bartolomeo di Giovanni, Franciabigio, Davide Ghirlandajo, Domenico Ghirlandajo, Giovanni di Francesco, Giovanni dal Ponte, Filippino Lippi, Machiavelli, Maso di Banco, Pesellino, Piero di Cosimo, Sogliani.

Charleston (South Carolina). GIBBES ART GALLERY: Unidentified Florentine 1465–1540.

Charlotte (North Carolina). MINT MUSEUM OF ART: Ridolfo Ghirlandajo, Granacci.
  MRS. GEORGE C. ADAMS: Giovanni del Biondo.

Charlottesville (Virginia). MRS. JOHN T. WESTLAKE: Sellajo.

Chartres. MUSÉE DES BEAUX-ARTS: Albertinelli, Domenico di Michelino.

Châteauroux (Indre). MUSÉE BERTRAND: Mariotto di Nardo.

Cherbourg. MUSÉE THOMAS HENRY: Botticelli, Francesco di Antonio, Mainardi, Master of the Castello Nativity.

Chianciano (Chiusi). MUNICIPIO: Lorenzo di Niccolò.
  COLLEGIATA: Puligo.

Chicago. ART INSTITUTE: Apollonio di Giovanni, Bartolomeo di Giovanni, Botticelli, Botticini, Bronzino, Daddi, Ridolfo Ghirlandajo, Jacopo di Cione, Master of the Bambino Vispo, Niccolò di Pietro Gerini, Sellajo, Spinello Aretino.

Chilston Park. VISCOUNTESS CHILSTON (EX): Raffaellino del Garbo.

Cincinnati (Ohio). ART MUSEUM: Apollonio di Giovanni, Botticini, Bronzino, Lorenzo di Credi.
  MR. AND MRS. IRWIN SIGNER: Puligo.

Città di Castello. PINACOTECA CIVICA: Domenico Ghirlandajo, Granacci, Neri di Bicci, Puligo, Spinello Aretino.
  DUOMO: Rosso Fiorentino.

Claremont (Cal.). POMONA COLLEGE: Neri di Bicci, Unidentified Florentine 1350–1420.

Cleveland (Ohio). MUSEUM OF ART: Andrea del Sarto, Botticini, Jacopo del Casentino, Filippino Lippi, Lorenzo di Credi, Lorenzo Monaco, Neri di Bicci, Pseudo Pier Francesco Fiorentino, Rosselli, Rossello di Jacopo, Sellajo, Unidentified Florentine 1420–1465.

Colle Val d'Elsa. MUSEO CIVICO: Pier Francesco Fiorentino.
  PALAZZO VESCOVILE: Pollajuolo.

Colle Val d'Elsa (*contd.*) S. AGOSTINO: Ridolfo Ghirlandajo.

   S. MARIA IN CANONICA: Pier Francesco Fiorentino.

   VIA GOZZINA: Pier Francesco Fiorentino.

   VIA DELLA PIEVE DEL PIANO: Pier Francesco Fiorentino.

Colle Ramole see Florence, Environs.

Cologne. WALLRAF RICHARTZ MUSEUM: Daddi, Francesco di Antonio, Mainardi, Neri di Bicci, Rosselli.

Colorado Springs (Colo.). FINE ARTS CENTER: Niccolò di Pietro Gerini.

Columbia (Mo.). UNIVERSITY OF MISSOURI: Alunno di Benozzo.

Columbia (South Carolina). MUSEUM OF ART: Albertinelli, Botticelli, Daddi, Giovanni dal Ponte, Rosselli.

Columbus (Ohio). GALLERY OF FINE ARTS: Pseudo Pier Francesco Fiorentino, Puligo.

Compton Wynyates (Warwicks.). MARQUESS OF NORTHAMPTON: Master of the Bambino Vispo.

Copenhagen. ROYAL MUSEUM: Andrea di Giusto, Bugiardini, Francesco di Antonio, Jacopo di Cione, Filippino Lippi, Lorenzo di Credi, Lorenzo Monaco, Mainardi, Spinello Aretino.

   THORWALDSEN MUSEUM: Lorenzo Monaco.

   AMALIENBORG PALACE: Sogliani.

Coral Gables (Flo.). UNIVERSITY OF MIAMI, JOE AND EMILY LOWE ART GALLERY: Andrea del Sarto, Bachiacca, Lorenzo di Credi, Puligo.

Corazzano (S. Miniato al Tedesco). S. GIOVANNI: Neri di Bicci.

Cori (Lazio). SS. ANNUNZIATA: Unidentified Florentine 1420–1465.

Cornbury Park (Charlbury, Oxon.). OLIVER VERNON WATNEY: Bachiacca, Botticelli.

Corsham Court (Wilts.). LORD METHUEN: Granacci, Filippo Lippi, Pesellino.

Cortona. ACCADEMIA ETRUSCA: Neri di Bicci.

   MUSEO DIOCESANO (CHIESA DEL GESÙ): Fra Angelico.

   PALAZZONE, CONTE PASSERINI: Master of S. Miniato.

   S. DOMENICO: Fra Angelico, Lorenzo di Niccolò.

   S. FRANCESCO: Spinello Aretino.

Cracow. CZARTORYSKI MUSEUM: Andrea da Firenze, Daddi, Giovanni dal Ponte, Gozzoli, Leonardo da Vinci, Master of S. Cecilia, Master of S. Miniato, Niccolò di Pietro Gerini, 'Tommaso', 'Utili', Unidentified Florentine 1420–1465.

   WAWEL MONASTERY: Mainardi.

Crespina (Pisa). S. MICHELE: Daddi.

Dallas (Texas). ART MUSEUM: Giusto d'Andrea.

Darmstadt. HESSISCHES LANDESMUSEUM: Bicci di Lorenzo (EX), Granacci.

Dayton (Ohio). ART INSTITUTE: Pontormo.

Denver (Colorado). MUSEUM OF ART: Alunno di Benozzo, Francesco di Antonio, Jacopo di Cione, Filippino Lippi, Lorenzo di Niccolò, Mainardi, Neri di Bicci, Niccolò di Pietro Gerini, Pesellino.

Detroit. INSTITUTE OF ARTS: Albertinelli, Fra Angelico, Bartolomeo di Giovanni, Botticelli, Bronzino, Franciabigio, Domenico Ghirlandajo, Giovanni del Biondo, Giovanni di Francesco, Mariotto di Nardo, Master of S. Cecilia, Master of S. Miniato, Neri di Bicci, Pseudo Pier Francesco Fiorentino, Unidentified Florentine 1420–1465.

Fabriano. PINACOTECA CIVICA: Bicci di Lorenzo.

   VESCOVADO: Neri di Bicci.

Faenza. PINACOTECA: Bronzino, 'Utili'.

   DUOMO: 'Utili'.

Faltugnano (Val di Bisenzio). SS. GIUSTO E CLEMENTE: Master of the Castello Nativity.

Faulkner (Md.). LOYOLA RETREAT HOUSE: Raffaellino del Garbo.

Fécamp. MUSÉE DE PEINTURE: 'Tommaso'.

Fiesole. MUSEO BANDINI: Andrea di Giusto, Bicci di Lorenzo, Cristiani, Daddi, Agnolo
   Gaddi, Taddeo Gaddi, Giovanni dal Ponte, Giusto d'Andrea, Jacopo di Cione,
   Lorenzo Monaco, Mariotto di Nardo, Master of S. Miniato, Michele di Ridolfo,
   Neri di Bicci, Niccolò di Pietro Gerini, Niccolò di Tommaso, Sellajo.

   DUOMO: Bicci di Lorenzo, Giovanni del Biondo, Rosselli.

   S. FRANCESCO: Neri di Bicci, Piero di Cosimo, Raffaellino del Garbo.

   S. MARIA PRIMERANA: Baldovinetti.

   VILLA LIMONAIA, MAX RUDOLF VON BUCH: Bronzino.

   CONTE COMM. RIGOLI: Alunno di Benozzo.

   VILLA DOCCIA: Raffaellino del Garbo.

   (Environs). ORATORIO DI FONTELUCENTE: Mariotto di Nardo.

   — VIA BENEDETTO DA MAJANO E VIA DEL SALVIATINO: 'Utili'.

Fifield House (Oxon.). MRS. LOUISE BISHOP (EX): Giovanni dal Ponte.

Figline (Valdarno Superiore): S. ANDREA A RIPALTA: Andrea di Giusto.

   S. FRANCESCO (MISERICORDIA): Francesco di Antonio, Giovanni del Biondo, Pier Francesco
   Fiorentino.

   — CONVENTO: Antonio Veneziano.

   S. PIETRO A TERRENO: Bugiardini.

Firenzuola (Mugello). MUNICIPIO: Giusto d'Andrea.

Firle Place (Lewes, Sussex). VISCOUNTESS GAGE: Fra Bartolommeo, Ridolfo Ghirlandajo,
   Puligo.

Florence. Galleries, Museums, Palazzi etc.

   GALLERIE FIORENTINE: Andrea del Sarto, Bachiacca, Fra Bartolommeo, Bartolomeo di
   Giovanni, Bicci di Lorenzo, Botticelli, Botticini, Bronzino, Bugiardini, Daddi,
   Franciabigio, Agnolo Gaddi, Domenico Ghirlandajo, Ridolfo Ghirlandajo, Giovanni
   del Biondo, Giovanni di Francesco, Giovanni dal Ponte, Giusto d'Andrea, Gozzoli,
   Filippino Lippi, Lorenzo di Credi, Lorenzo di Niccolò, Mainardi, Mariotto di Nardo,
   Master of the Bambino Vispo, Michele di Ridolfo, Neri di Bicci, Niccolò di Tom-
   maso, Fra Paolino, Pontormo, Raffaellino del Garbo, Rosselli, Rossello di Jacopo,
   Sellajo, Sogliani, 'Utili'.

   GALLERIA DELL'ACCADEMIA: Albertinelli, Andrea da Firenze, Andrea di Giusto, Baldo-
   vinetti, Fra Bartolommeo, Bartolomeo di Giovanni, Bicci di Lorenzo, Botticelli,
   Botticini, Bronzino, Cristiani, Daddi, Francesco di Antonio, Franciabigio, Agnolo
   Gaddi, Taddeo Gaddi, Ridolfo Ghirlandajo, Giotto Follower, Giovanni del Biondo,
   Giovanni di Francesco, Giovanni da Milano, Giovanni dal Ponte, Giusto d'Andrea,
   Granacci, Jacopo del Casentino, Jacopo di Cione, Filippino Lippi, Lorenzo di Credi,
   Lorenzo Monaco, Lorenzo di Niccolò, Mainardi, Mariotto di Cristofano, Mariotto di
   Nardo, Master of the Arte della Lana Coronation, Master of the Bambino Vispo,
   Master of the Castello Nativity, Master of the Rinuccini Chapel, Michelangelo,

Michele di Ridolfo, Nardo di Cione, Neri di Bicci, Niccolò di Pietro Gerini, Niccolò di Tommaso, Orcagna, Pacino di Bonaguida, Pseudo Pier Francesco Fiorentino, Pontormo, Puccio di Simone, Raffaellino del Garbo, Rosselli, Rossello di Jacopo, Sellajo, Sogliani, Spinello Aretino, Unidentified Florentine 1350–1420, Unidentified Florentine 1420–1465.

GALLERIA DEGLI UFFIZI: Albertinelli, Andrea del Sarto, Fra Angelico, Bachiacca, Baldovinetti, Bartolomeo di Giovanni, Botticelli, Botticini, Bronzino, Cimabue, Daddi, Domenico Veneziano, Franciabigio, Taddeo Gaddi, Domenico Ghirlandajo, Giotto, Giovanni da Milano, Giovanni dal Ponte, Gozzoli, Granacci, Jacopo del Casentino, Jacopo di Cione, Leonardo da Vinci, Filippino Lippi, Filippo Lippi, Lorenzo di Credi, Lorenzo Monaco, Masaccio, Master of S. Cecilia, Michelangelo, Nardo di Cione, Pesellino, Pseudo Pier Francesco Fiorentino, Piero di Cosimo, Pollajuolo, Pontormo, Puligo, Rosselli, Rosso Fiorentino, Sellajo, Spinello Aretino, Uccello, Verrocchio.

— GABINETTO DEI DISEGNI: Andrea del Sarto, Pontormo.

GALLERIA PALATINA DI PALAZZO PITTI: Albertinelli, Andrea del Sarto, Bachiacca, Fra Bartolommeo, Botticelli, Botticini, Bronzino, Bugiardini, Franciabigio, Ridolfo Ghirlandajo, Granacci, Filippino Lippi, Filippo Lippi, Michele di Ridolfo, Fra Paolino, Pseudo Pier Francesco Fiorentino, Piero di Cosimo, Pontormo, Puligo, Rosso Fiorentino, Sellajo, 'Tommaso'.

MUSEO BARDINI: Bugiardini, Agnolo Gaddi, Lorenzo di Niccolò, Master of S. Miniato, Pseudo Pier Francesco Fiorentino, Pollajuolo.

BARGELLO, CAPPELLA DEL PODESTÀ O DELLA MADDALENA: Giotto Assistant.

— MUSEO NAZIONALE: Alunno di Benozzo, Bronzino, Agnolo Gaddi, Taddeo Gaddi, Giovanni di Francesco, Lorenzo Monaco, Lorenzo di Niccolò, Mainardi, Master of the Arte della Lana Coronation, Michelangelo, Pseudo Pier Francesco Fiorentino, Pollajuolo, Raffaellino del Garbo, Rossello di Jacopo, Verrocchio, Unidentified Florentine 1350–1420.

MUSEO DEL BIGALLO: Alunno di Benozzo, Daddi, Giusto d'Andrea, Jacopo di Cione, Master of the Bambino Vispo, Master of S. Miniato, Niccolò di Pietro Gerini, Rossello di Jacopo, Sellajo.

MUSEO DEL CASTAGNO (CENACOLO DI S. APOLLONIA): Castagno, Davide Ghirlandajo, Paolo Schiavo, Pier Francesco Fiorentino.

MUSEO FERRONI (CENACOLO DI FOLIGNO): Filippino Lippi, Lorenzo Monaco, Fra Paolino.

MUSEO HORNE: Bartolomeo di Giovanni, Daddi, Francesco di Antonio, Franciabigio, Taddeo Gaddi, Giotto, Giotto Follower, Giovanni dal Ponte, Gozzoli, Jacopo del Casentino, Filippino Lippi, Lorenzo Monaco, Masaccio, Master of the Bambino Vispo, Master of S. Cecilia, Neri di Bicci, Niccolò di Tommaso, Pseudo Pier Francesco Fiorentino, Piero di Cosimo, Sellajo, 'Tommaso'.

MUSEO DI S. CROCE, S. MARCO, S. MARIA DEL FIORE (DUOMO): see Churches.

MUSEO DELL'OPERA DEL DUOMO, see Churches, S. Maria del Fiore.

MUSEO STIBBERT: Andrea di Giusto, Bronzino, Benedetto Ghirlandajo, Granacci, Jacopo di Cione, Mariotto di Nardo, Neri di Bicci, Rosselli, Unidentified Florentine 1420–1465'

ARCHIVIO NOTARILE: Taddeo Gaddi, Sogliani.

BIBLIOTECA LAURENZIANA: Andrea di Giusto, Lorenzo Monaco.

BIBLIOTECA RICCARDIANA: Apollonio di Giovanni.

Florence (*contd.*) CASA BUONARROTI: Bugiardini, Giovanni di Francesco, Michelangelo.

COMPAGNIA DEL BIGALLO: Mariotto di Nardo.

CONSERVATORIO, see Churches, S. Maria degli Angeli.

EDUCATORIO DI FOLIGNO (GIÀ CHIOSTRO): Bicci di Lorenzo.

/ PALAZZO DELL'ARCIVESCOVADO: Filippo Lippi.

PALAZZO DELL'ARTE DELLA LANA: Jacopo del Casentino, Master of the Arte della Lana Coronation.

PALAZZO DEL BARGELLO see Bargello, above.

PALAZZO DELLA CASSA DI RISPARMIO: Nardo di Cione.

PALAZZO DAVANZATI: Bachiacca, Francesco di Antonio, Franciabigio, Granacci, Piero di Cosimo, Rossello di Jacopo.

PALAZZO DI PARTE GUELFA: 'Utili'.

PALAZZO GUICCIARDINI (EX): Pontormo.

PALAZZO RICCARDI (MUSEO MEDICEO): Bronzino, Domenico Ghirlandajo, Ridolfo Ghirlandajo, Gozzoli, Granacci, Filippo Lippi, Pseudo Pier Francesco Fiorentino, Pontormo.

PALAZZO VECCHIO: Bachiacca, Bartolomeo di Giovanni, Botticelli, Bronzino, Cimabue, Davide Ghirlandajo, Domenico Ghirlandajo, Ridolfo Ghirlandajo, Jacopo di Cione, Leonardo da Vinci, Michelangelo, Pontormo, Rosselli, Rossello di Jacopo, Sellajo, Verrocchio.

TABERNACLES: LUNGARNO SODERINI: Sellajo.

— PIAZZA S. MARIA NOVELLA: Francesco di Antonio.

— PORTA S. GIORGIO: Bicci di Lorenzo.

— VIA DEGLI ALFANI E BORGO PINTI: Daddi.

— VIA RICASOLI: Rosselli.

— VIA ROMANA: Master of S. Miniato.

— VIA SAN ZANOBI E VIA DELLE RUOTE: Puligo.

— VIA SERRAGLI E VIA S. MONICA: Bicci di Lorenzo.

— VIA DEI TAVOLINI: Giovanni dal Ponte.

Florence. Churches.

DUOMO, see S. Maria del Fiore.

S. AGATA: Lorenzo di Credi.

S. AMBROGIO: Baldovinetti, Bicci di Lorenzo, Cristiani, Agnolo Gaddi, Filippino Lippi, Raffaellino del Garbo, Rosselli.

SS. ANNUNZIATA: Andrea del Sarto, Baldovinetti, Botticelli, Bronzino, Castagno, Franciabigio, Pontormo, Raffaellino del Garbo, Rosselli, Rosso Fiorentino, Sogliani, 'Tommaso'.

S. APOLLONIA, see Museo del Castagno.

SS. APOSTOLI: Orcagna.

BADIA: Bronzino, Filippino Lippi, Maso di Banco, Master of the Castello Nativity, Nardo di Cione.

S. BARNABA: Spinello Aretino.

BATTISTERO: Cimabue.

COMPAGNIA DI S. BONIFACIO, CAPPELLA: Giotto Contemporary.

S. CARLO DEI LOMBARDI: Niccolò di Pietro Gerini.

CARMINE, see S. Maria del Carmine.

S. CROCE: Bicci di Lorenzo, Daddi, Agnolo Gaddi, Taddeo Gaddi, Davide Ghirlandajo, Giotto, Giotto Assistant, Giotto Follower, Giovanni del Biondo, Giovanni da Milano, Giusto d'Andrea, Jacopo di Cione, Lorenzo di Niccolò, Mainardi, Mariotto di Nardo, Maso di Banco, Master of the Rinuccini Chapel, Nardo di Cione, Neri di Bicci, Niccolò di Pietro Gerini, Spinello Aretino, Unidentified Florentine 1420-1465.

— MUSEO DELL'OPERA: Bronzino, Bugiardini, Cimabue, Domenico Veneziano, Giotto Assistant, Giovanni da Milano, Lorenzo Monaco, Maso di Banco, Master of the Bambino Vispo, Michele di Ridolfo, Orcagna, Sogliani, Spinello Aretino.

S. FELICE: Botticelli, Giotto Assistant, Michele di Ridolfo, Neri di Bicci.

S. FELICITA: Bicci di Lorenzo, Bronzino, Francesco di Antonio, Taddeo Gaddi, Giovanni del Biondo, Lorenzo di Niccolò, Master of the Castello Nativity, Neri di Bicci, Niccolò di Pietro Gerini, Pontormo.

S. FIRENZE: Bachiacca.

S. FREDIANO: Sellajo.

S. GIORGIO ALLA COSTA: Master of S. Cecilia.

S. GIOVANNINO DEI CAVALIERI: Bicci di Lorenzo, Granacci, Lorenzo Monaco, Master of the Castello Nativity, Neri di Bicci, Pseudo Pier Francesco Fiorentino.

S. GIOVANNINO DELLA CALZA: Franciabigio.

S. GIUSEPPE: Lorenzo Monaco, Raffaellino del Garbo, Sogliani.

INNOCENTI: see Spedale degli Innocenti and S. Maria degli Innocenti.

S. JACOPO IN CAMPO CORBOLINI: Davide Ghirlandajo.

S. JACOPO SOPRARNO: Sellajo.

S. LEONARDO IN ARCETRI: Lorenzo di Niccolò, Neri di Bicci.

S. LORENZO: Bronzino, Davide Ghirlandajo, Domenico Ghirlandajo, Ridolfo Ghirlandajo, Filippo Lippi, Michelangelo, Piero di Cosimo, Rosso Fiorentino, Sogliani, Verrocchio.

S. LUCIA DEI MAGNOLI (TRA LE ROVINATE): Sellajo.

S. LUCIA AL PRATO: Maso di Banco.

S. MARCO: Fra Bartolommeo, Giotto Follower.

— MUSEO DI SAN MARCO: Albertinelli, Andrea di Giusto, Andrea del Sarto, Fra Angelico, Baldovinetti, Fra Bartolommeo, Domenico di Michelino, Taddeo Gaddi, Domenico Ghirlandajo, Lorenzo Monaco, Fra Paolino, Rosselli, Sogliani, Strozzi.

S. MARGHERITA DEI RICCI: Neri di Bicci, Pesellino.

S. MARIA DEGLI ANGELI: Ridolfo Ghirlandajo, Giusto d'Andrea.

S. MARIA DEL CARMINE: Andrea da Firenze, Bicci di Lorenzo, Filippino Lippi, Filippo Lippi, Masaccio, Masolino, Unidentified Florentine 1350-1420.

S. MARIA DEL FIORE: Baldovinetti, Bicci di Lorenzo, Castagno, Daddi, Domenico di Michelino, Domenico Ghirlandajo, Giotto Follower, Giovanni del Biondo, Lorenzo di Credi, Michelangelo, Rossello di Jacopo, Sogliani, Uccello.

— OPERA DEL DUOMO: Baldovinetti, Bicci di Lorenzo, Daddi, Giovanni del Biondo, Jacopo del Casentino, Pollajuolo, Verrocchio, Unidentified Florentine 1420-1465.

S. MARIA DEGLI INNOCENTI: Albertinelli, Giovanni di Francesco, Sogliani.

S. MARIA MAGGIORE: Giovanni di Francesco, Spinello Aretino.

S. MARIA NOVELLA: Botticelli, Bronzino, Cimabue, Benedetto Ghirlandajo, Davide Ghirlandajo, Domenico Ghirlandajo, Giotto, Jacopo del Casentino, Mainardi, Masaccio, Neri di Bicci.

Florence. S. MARIA NOVELLA (*contd.*) CAPPELLA BARDI: Spinello Aretino.
— CAPPELLA DEL PAPA: Ridolfo Ghirlandajo, Pontormo.
— CAPPELLA RUCELLAI: Bugiardini.
— CAPPELLONE DEGLI SPAGNUOLI: Andrea da Firenze, Daddi.
— CAPPELLA STROZZI: Giovanni del Biondo, Jacopo di Cione, Filippino Lippi, Nardo di Cione, Orcagna.
— CHIOSTRINO DEI MORTI: Jacopo di Cione, Nardo di Cione.
— CHIOSTRO VERDE: Uccello, Unidentified Florentine 1420–1465.
— CONVENTO: Unidentified Florentine 1465–1540.
— EX-REFETTORIO: Agnolo Gaddi.
— FARMACIA: Mariotto di Nardo.
S. MARIA MADDALENA DEI PAZZI: Puligo, Raffaellino del Garbo, Rosselli.
S. MARTINO ALLA SCALA: Botticelli, Granacci, Uccello.
S. MARTINO BUONOMINI: Benedetto Ghirlandajo, Davide Ghirlandajo.
S. MICHELE A SAN SALVI: Raffaellino del Garbo.
S. MICHELE VISDOMINI: Pontormo.
S. MINIATO AL MONTE: Baldovinetti, Castagno, Agnolo Gaddi, Taddeo Gaddi, Jacopo del Casentino, Mariotto di Nardo, Paolo Schiavo, Pollajuolo, Rossello di Jacopo, Spinello Aretino, Uccello, Unidentified Florentine 1420–1465.
S. NICCOLÒ: Bicci di Lorenzo, Neri di Bicci, Pollajuolo.
S. NICCOLÒ DEL CEPPO: Sogliani.
S. NICCOLÒ OLTRARNO: Francesco di Antonio.
EX-CONVENTO DELLE OBLATE: Lorenzo Monaco.
OGNISSANTI: Botticelli, Taddeo Gaddi, Davide Ghirlandajo, Domenico Ghirlandajo, Giotto Follower, Giovanni del Biondo, Lorenzo Monaco, Master of S. Miniato, Nardo di Cione, Unidentified Florentine 1420–1465.
ORSANMICHELE (S. MICHELE IN ORTO): Daddi, Giovanni dal Ponte, Lorenzo di Credi, Niccolò di Pietro Gerini, Orcagna, Sogliani, Verrocchio.
S. PANCRAZIO: Baldovinetti, Neri di Bicci.
S. PROCOLO: Raffaellino del Garbo.
REGINA DELLA PACE: Bronzino.
S. SALVATORE AL MONTE: Giovanni dal Ponte, Neri di Bicci.
CENACOLO DI SAN SALVI: Andrea del Sarto, Puligo, Sogliani, 'Tommaso'.
CHIOSTRO DELLO SCALZO: Andrea del Sarto, Franciabigio.
S. SEBASTIANO DEI BINI: Rossello di Jacopo, Sogliani.
S. SIMONE: Master of S. Cecilia.
S. SPIRITO: Bartolomeo di Giovanni, Botticini, Granacci, Filippino Lippi, Michele di Ridolfo, Neri di Bicci, Raffaellino del Garbo, Rosselli, Sellajo, 'Tommaso'.
— CENACOLO DI S. SPIRITO: Maso di Banco.
SS. STEFANO E CECILIA: Nardo di Cione.
S. TRINITA: Baldovinetti, Bicci di Lorenzo, Daddi, Francesco di Antonio, Davide Ghirlandajo, Domenico Ghirlandajo, Ridolfo Ghirlandajo, Giovanni di Francesco, Giovanni dal Ponte, Jacopo di Cione, Lorenzo Monaco, Mariotto di Nardo, Michele di Ridolfo, Neri di Bicci.
ORATORIO DELLE STIMMATE (SAN LORENZO): Pseudo Pier Francesco Fiorentino.
SEMINARIO MAGGIORE: Giovanni di Francesco, Masolino.

SPEDALE DEGLI INNOCENTI: Bartolomeo di Giovanni, Botticelli, Domenico Ghirlandajo, Giovanni del Biondo, Neri di Bicci, Piero di Cosimo, Pontormo, Puligo, Rossello di Jacopo, Rosso Fiorentino, Unidentified Florentine 1350–1420.

SPEDALE DI ORBATELLO: Domenico Ghirlandajo, Mainardi, Master of S. Miniato.

SPEDALE DI S. MARIA NUOVA: Bicci di Lorenzo, Castagno.

Florence. Private Collections.

ACTON COLLECTION: Cristiani, Daddi, Lippo di Benivieni, Mariotto di Nardo, Master of S. Miniato, Niccolò di Tommaso.

BARTOLINI SALIMBENI COLLECTION: 'Utili'.

BERENSON COLLECTION: Andrea di Giusto, Bachiacca, Daddi, Domenico Veneziano, Giotto, Giotto Assistant, Giotto Follower, Giovanni da Milano, Granacci, Jacopo di Cione, Lorenzo Monaco, Master of the Castello Nativity, Nardo di Cione, Neri di Bicci, Pesellino, 'Utili'.

CONTE FERRANTE CAPPONE: Pontormo.

CINELLI COLLECTION (EX): Orcagna.

CONTINI BONACOSSI COLLECTION: Bachiacca, Fra Bartolommeo, Botticelli, Castagno, Cimabue, Agnolo Gaddi, Ridolfo Ghirlandajo, Giovanni del Biondo, Giovanni di Francesco, Giovanni da Milano, Master of S. Cecilia, Pontormo, Rosselli, Unidentified Florentine 1420–1465.

GALLERIA CORSINI: Andrea del Sarto, Botticelli, Ridolfo Ghirlandajo, Filippino Lippi, Pontormo, Puligo, Sellajo, Tommaso di Stefano Lunetti.

PRINCIPE TOMMASO CORSINI: Strozzi.

MRS. C. H. COSTER: Alunno di Benozzo, Francesco di Antonio, Mainardi.

CONTE COSIMO DEGLI ALESSANDRI: Lippo di Benivieni.

CHARLES LOESER (EX): Andrea di Giusto, Antonio Veneziano, Daddi, Jacopo del Casentino, Master of S. Cecilia, Neri di Bicci, Niccolò di Pietro Gerini.

PROF. ROBERTO LONGHI: Mariotto di Nardo.

RICHARD MAYO: Master of S. Miniato.

MARCHESE MANNELLI RICCARDI (EX): Bartolomeo di Giovanni.

CONTE VITTORIO DE MICHELI: Jacopo del Casentino.

FAIRFAX MURRAY (EX): Unidentified Florentine 1465–1540.

MARCHESE NICCOLINI: Bachiacca.

MARCHESA BEATRICE ROSSELLI DEL TURCO: Sellajo.

MARCHESE SERLUPI-CRESCENZI: Franciabigio.

SERRISTORI COLLECTION: Bachiacca (EX), Daddi, Mariotto di Nardo, Master of S. Miniato, Neri di Bicci, Sogliani.

MARCHESA LUCIA TORRIGIANI: Ridolfo Ghirlandajo.

H. BLAKISTON WILKINS (EX): Cristiani, Franciabigio.

Florence. Environs.

ANTELLA, ORATORIO DI S. CATERINA: Spinello Aretino.

BADIA FIESOLANA: Botticelli.

BADIA A SETTIMO see Settimo.

BAGNO A RIPOLI, S. MARIA DI QUARTO: Bicci di Lorenzo, Cristiani, Daddi.

BOLDRONE: Pontormo.

BROZZI, S. ANDREA: Botticini, Domenico Ghirlandajo, Master of the Bambino Vispo, Raffaellino del Garbo.

Florence (Environs). BROZZI (*contd.*) S. LUCIA ALLA SALA: Paolo Schiavo.

— VIA DI BROZZI E VIA PISTOIESE: Mainardi.

BRUCIANESI, MADONNA DI FATIMA: Master of S. Miniato.

CALDINE, S. MARIA MADDALENA: Fra Bartolommeo, Bicci di Lorenzo, Master of S. Cecilia.

CAREGGI, S. PIETRO: Giusto d'Andrea.

— NUOVO CONVENTO DELLE OBLATE: Lorenzo Monaco, Niccolò di Tommaso.

CARMIGNANO, PIEVE: Pontormo.

CASTELLO, S. MICHELE: Sellajo, Unidentified Florentine 1350–1420.

— TABERNACOLO DELL'OLMO: Paolo Schiavo.

CERTOSA DEL GALLUZZO: Albertinelli, Bronzino, Giovanni dal Ponte, Mariotto di Nardo, Michele di Ridolfo, Orcagna, Pontormo, Raffaellino del Garbo, Unidentified Florentine 1420–1465.

COLLE RAMOLE see Villa Agostini.

CONVENTO DEL BOSCO AI FRATI (CAFAGGIOLO): Sogliani.

CORBIGNANO, CAPPELLA VANELLA: Botticelli.

IMPRUNETA, COLLEGIATA: Mariotto di Nardo, Unidentified Florentine 1350–1420.

LA QUIETE (CONVENTO DELLE MONTALVE): Botticelli, Ridolfo Ghirlandajo, Master of the Bambino Vispo, Michele di Ridolfo.

LEGNAIA, S. ARCANGELO: Bicci di Lorenzo, Mariotto di Nardo.

LE SIECI, S. GIOVANNI A REMOLE: Botticelli.

MONTICELLI, S. MARIA DELLA QUERCE: Paolo Schiavo.

PARADISO DEGLI ALBERTI: Niccolò di Pietro Gerini.

PATERNO, S. STEFANO: Cimabue.

PERETOLA, S. MARIA: Giusto d'Andrea.

PETRIOLO, S. BIAGIO: Giovanni di Francesco.

POGGIO A CAIANO see Villa Medicea.

PONTE A GREVE: Bicci di Lorenzo.

POZZOLATICO, S. STEFANO: Jacopo del Casentino.

QUINTOLE, S. PIETRO: Granacci.

ROVEZZANO, VIA DEL GUARLONE E VIA DEL RONDININO: Raffaellino del Garbo.

S. ANDREA A BOTINACCIO, CHIESA DI S. MARIA COELI AULA: Machiavelli.

S. ANDREA A CERCINA: Domenico Ghirlandajo, Nardo di Cione.

S. BARTOLOMEO A QUARATA: Rosso Fiorentino.

S. BRIGIDA ALL'OPACO: Unidentified Florentine 1350–1420.

S. DOMENICO DI FIESOLE: Fra Angelico, Botticelli, Lorenzo di Credi, Rossello di Jacopo, Sogliani.

S. DONNINO DI VILLAMAGNA: Davide Ghirlandajo, Granacci, Mariotto di Nardo.

S. FELICE A EMA: Giovanni del Biondo.

S. GIORGIO A RUBALLA: Daddi, Taddeo Gaddi.

S. LORENZO IN COLLINA: Lorenzo di Niccolò.

S. LORENZO ALLE ROSE: Taddeo Gaddi.

S. MARGHERITA A MONTICI: Master of S. Cecilia.

S. MARIA A QUINTO: Lorenzo di Niccolò, Spinello, Unidentified Florentine 1350–1420.

S. MARIA A SAN MARTINO ALLA PALMA: Michele di Ridolfo.

S. MARTINO A GANGALANDI: Bicci di Lorenzo, Lorenzo Monaco, Michele di Ridolfo, Sellajo.

S. MARTINO A MENSOLA: Taddeo Gaddi, Machiavelli, Neri di Bicci.

s. MARTINO ALLA PALMA: Unidentified Florentine 1350–1420.

s. MARTINO A SESTO: Cenni di Francesco, Agnolo Gaddi.

s. MARTINO A STRADA: 'Utili'.

s. MARTINO A TERENZANO: Lorenzo di Niccolò, Pietro di Miniato.

SETTIMO, s. ROMOLO: Lorenzo Monaco.

— BADIA DI s. SALVATORE: Sellajo.

SIGNANO, s. GIUSTO: Daddi.

TORRE DEGLI AGLI: Antonio Veneziano.

TORRE DEL GALLO: Pollajuolo.

VIA DI BOLDRONE: Pontormo.

VICCHIO DI RIMAGGIO, s. LORENZO: Mariotto di Nardo, Master of S. Cecilia, Pietro di Miniato.

VILLA AGOSTINI A COLLE RAMOLE: Ridolfo Ghirlandajo.

VILLA LE CAMPORA: Unidentified Florentine 1350–1420.

VILLA CAPPONI AD ARCETRI: Tommaso di Stefano Lunetti.

VILLA CARDUCCI PANDOLFINI A LEGNAIA: Castagno.

VILLA MEDICEA, POGGIO A CAIANO: Andrea del Sarto, Franciabigio, Filippino Lippi, Pontormo, Unidentified Florentine 1465–1540.

VILLA SCHIFANOIA: Lorenzo di Credi, Pseudo Pier Francesco Fiorentino, 'Tommaso'.

VILLA SPARTA: 'Tommaso'.

VINCIGLIATA, CASTELLO: Bicci di Lorenzo (EX), Mariotto di Nardo.

— s. LORENZO: Niccolò di Pietro Gerini.

Foligno. MISERICORDIA: Neri di Bicci.

Fontainebleau. CHÂTEAU: Rosso Fiorentino.

Fontanellato (Parma). CASTELLO: Pesellino.

Forlì. PINACOTECA COMUNALE: Lorenzo di Credi, Unidentified Florentine 1350–1420.

Frankfurt am Main. STAEDELSCHES KUNSTINSTITUT: Fra Angelico, Botticelli, Fra Diamante, Jacopo del Casentino, Master of the Bambino Vispo, Pseudo Pier Francesco Fiorentino, Pontormo, Rosso Fiorentino, Verrocchio.

GEORG HARTMANN: Neri di Bicci.

Fucecchio (Valdarno). MUSEO: Machiavelli.

COLLEGIATA (s. GIOVANNI BATTISTA): Francesco di Antonio, Michele di Ridolfo.

Gaviserri (Stia, Casentino). s. ANDREA CORSINI: Master of S. Miniato.

Gazzada (Varese). VILLA CAGNOLA: Giovanni del Biondo, Jacopo di Cione, Rosselli.

Geneva. MUSÉE D'ART ET D'HISTOIRE: Albertinelli, Alunno di Benozzo, Fra Bartolommeo, Jacopo di Cione.

VILLA ARIANA: Jacopo del Casentino.

Genoa. PALAZZO BIANCO: Franciabigio, Filippino Lippi, Pontormo, Puligo.

ALESSANDRO BASEVI: Albertinelli.

VIEZZOLI COLLECTION: Master of the Bambino Vispo.

(Environs). PEGLI, MUSEO NAVALE: Ridolfo Ghirlandajo.

Ghent. MUSÉE DES BEAUX ARTS: Daddi.

Glasgow. CORPORATION ART GALLERIES: Botticelli, Domenico Veneziano, Pseudo Pier Francesco Fiorentino, Raffaellino del Garbo.

Glen Falls (N.Y.). MRS. LOUIS HYDE: Botticelli (EX?).

Gosford House (Longniddry, Scotland). EARL OF WEMYSS AND MARCH: Albertinelli, Botticelli, 'Tommaso'.

Gotha. LANDESMUSEUM: Pontormo.

Göttingen. UNIVERSITY: Antonio Veneziano, Botticini, Daddi, Fra Diamante, Lorenzo di Credi, Lorenzo Monaco, Master of the Castello Nativity, Pseudo Pier Francesco Fiorentino, Sellajo.

Granada. ALHAMBRA: Unidentified Florentine 1420–1465.

   CAPILLA REAL: Botticelli.

Grand Rapids (Mich.). ART GALLERY: Mariotto di Nardo.

Graz. LANDESBILDERGALERIE, PALAIS ATTEMS: Lorenzo di Niccolò.

Greenville (South Carolina). BOB JONES UNIVERSITY: Bicci di Lorenzo, Master of S. Miniato, Michele di Ridolfo, Niccolò di Pietro Gerini.

Grenoble. MUSÉE DE PEINTURE: Francesco di Antonio, Neri di Bicci, Puligo.

Grey Walls (East Dean, Sussex). LADY SALMOND: Pontormo.

Grottaferrata (Rome). BADIA: Bicci di Lorenzo.

Gubbio. PINACOTECA: Pseudo Pier Francesco Fiorentino.

Habana (Cuba). OSCAR B. CINTAS: Rosselli.

The Hague. MAURITSHUIS: Albertinelli.

Halle. GALERIE: Rosselli.

Hamburg. KUNSTHALLE: Daddi (EX), Mainardi, Pontormo.

   GALERIE WEBER (EX): Botticelli, Franciabigio, Sogliani.

   WEDELLS COLLECTION (EX): Giovanni del Biondo.

Hampton Court. ROYAL COLLECTION: Andrea del Sarto, Fra Angelico, Daddi, Franciabigio, Jacopo di Cione, Mariotto di Nardo, Puligo, Sellajo.

Hanover. LANDESGALERIE: Antonio Veneziano, Apollonio di Giovanni, Botticelli, Giovanni dal Ponte, Lorenzo di Credi, Master of the Castello Nativity, Pontormo.

Harewood House (Yorks.). EARL OF HAREWOOD: Albertinelli.

Hartford (Conn.). WADSWORTH ATHENEUM: Fra Angelico, Bachiacca, Master of S. Miniato, Piero di Cosimo.

   TRINITY COLLEGE: Domenico Ghirlandajo.

Heemstede (Haarlem). BOSCHBECK, F. GUTMANN: Unidentified Florentine 1420–1465.

Helsinki. ATENEUM: Andrea di Giusto, Master of the Bambino Vispo.

High Hall (Wimborne, Dorset). MRS. ISABEL TRACEY: Sogliani.

Highnam Court (Glos.). GAMBIER PARRY COLLECTION: Albertinelli, Daddi, Francesco di Antonio, Agnolo Gaddi, Giovanni dal Ponte, Jacopo di Cione, Lorenzo Monaco, Lorenzo di Niccolò, Master of S. Miniato, Pesellino, Pseudo Pier Francesco Fiorentino, Rossello di Jacopo, Sellajo, Unidentified Florentine 1420–1465, Unidentified Florentine 1465–1540.

Hoe Hall (Dereham, Norfolk). MRS. JOSEPH BARCLAY (EX): Raffaellino del Garbo.

Holkham Hall (Norfolk). EARL OF LEICESTER: Michelangelo.

Honolulu. ACADEMY OF ARTS: Fra Diamante, Granacci, Piero di Cosimo.

Horsmonden (Kent). MRS. AUSTEN (EX): Bartolomeo di Giovanni.

Houston (Texas). MUSEUM OF FINE ARTS: Fra Angelico, Domenico Veneziano, Jacopo di Cione, Lorenzo Monaco, Raffaellino del Garbo, Rosselli, Unidentified Florentine 1350–1420.

Litchfield (Conn.). STANLEY MORTIMER: Granacci, Sellajo.

Little Rock (Arkansas). FINE ARTS CLUB. Cenni di Francesco.

Liverpool. WALKER ART GALLERY: Bartolomeo di Giovanni, Bicci di Lorenzo, Giovanni del Biondo, Granacci, Jacopo di Cione, Lorenzo di Credi, Neri di Bicci, Pseudo Pier Francesco Fiorentino, Rosselli, Rosso Fiorentino, Sogliani, Spinello Aretino, 'Utili'.

Livorno, see Leghorn.

Lockinge House (Wantage, Berks.). CHRISTOPHER LOYD: Botticelli, Pesellino.

Locko Park (Derbyshire). COL. J. PACKE-DRURY-LOWE: Bachiacca, Bartolomeo di Giovanni, Gozzoli, Raffaellino del Garbo.

London. NATIONAL GALLERY: Andrea del Sarto, Fra Angelico, Apollonio di Giovanni, Bachiacca, Baldovinetti, Fra Bartolommeo, Botticelli, Botticini, Bronzino, Castagno, Cristiani, Fra Diamante, Domenico di Michelino, Domenico Veneziano, Francesco di Antonio, Franciabigio, Agnolo Gaddi, Domenico Ghirlandajo, Ridolfo Ghirlandajo, Giotto Assistant, Giovanni di Francesco, Giovanni da Milano, Giovanni dal Ponte, Gozzoli, Granacci, Jacopo di Cione, Leonardo da Vinci, Filippino Lippi, Filippo Lippi, Lorenzo di Credi, Lorenzo Monaco, Machiavelli, Mainardi, Masaccio, Masolino, Master of the Bambino Vispo, Master of the Castello Nativity, Master of S. Miniato, Michelangelo, Nardo di Cione, Niccolò di Pietro Gerini, Pesellino, Pseudo Pier Francesco Fiorentino, Piero di Cosimo, Pollajuolo, Pontormo, Raffaellino del Garbo, Rosselli, Sellajo, Sogliani, Spinello Aretino, Uccello, Verrocchio, Unidentified Florentine 1350–1420.

BRITISH MUSEUM: Master of S. Miniato.

BURLINGTON HOUSE, ROYAL ACADEMY OF ARTS: Michelangelo.

DULWICH COLLEGE ART GALLERY, see Dulwich.

COURTAULD INSTITUTE GALLERIES: Botticelli, Daddi, Fra Diamante, Agnolo Gaddi, Giovanni dal Ponte, Master of the Castello Nativity, 'Utili', Unidentified Florentine 1350–1420.

VICTORIA AND ALBERT MUSEUM: Apollonio di Giovanni, Bartolomeo di Giovanni, Botticelli, Francesco di Antonio, Leonardo da Pistoia, Michelangelo, Nardo di Cione, Pier Francesco Fiorentino, Pseudo Pier Francesco Fiorentino, Verrocchio.

WALLACE COLLECTION: Andrea del Sarto, Daddi, Piero di Cosimo.

HATTON GARDEN CHURCH (EX): Mariotto di Nardo.

WESTMINSTER ABBEY: Bicci di Lorenzo.

BUCKINGHAM PALACE, ROYAL COLLECTION: Domenico di Michelino, Giovanni del Biondo, Gozzoli, Pesellino.

SIR THOMAS BARLOW: Fra Angelico, Rosselli.

SIR RICHARD BARRETT LENNARD: Lorenzo Monaco.

LORD BURTON (EX): Pontormo.

CHARLES BUTLER (EX): Unidentified Florentine 1420–1465.

LORD CARMICHAEL (EX): Master of the Bambino Vispo.

HENRY DOETSCH (EX): Bachiacca.

MARY DODGE (EX): Rossello di Jacopo.

SIR WILLIAM FARRER (EX): Puligo.

PETER FULD: Andrea di Giusto, Domenico Veneziano.

Lugano. SCHLOSS ROHONCZ COLLECTION (BARON H. THYSSEN): Fra Angelico, Fra Bartolommeo, Daddi, Domenico Veneziano, Domenico Ghirlandajo, Giovanni di Francesco, Gozzoli, Filippino Lippi, Master of the Bambino Vispo, Pseudo Pier Francesco Fiorentino, Pontormo, Sellajo, Unidentified Florentine 1350–1420.

Luton Hoo (Bedfordshire). SIR HAROLD WERNHER: Filippino Lippi, 'Tommaso'.

Lützschena (Leipzig). SPECK VON STERNBURG (EX): Mariotto di Nardo.

Lwów. MUSEUM: Pontormo.

PRINCE PININSKI (EX): Master of S. Miniato.

Lyon. MUSÉE DES BEAUX-ARTS: Giovanni di Francesco, Master of S. Miniato, 'Utili', Unidentified Florentine 1350–1420.

EDOUARD AYNARD (EX): Alunno di Benozzo, Master of the Bambino Vispo, Pesellino.

Madison (Wisc.). UNIVERSITY OF WISCONSIN: Rossello di Jacopo.

Madrid. MUSEO DEL PRADO: Andrea del Sarto, Fra Angelico, Bartolomeo di Giovanni, Botticelli, Giovanni dal Ponte.

DUKE OF ALBA: Albertinelli, Fra Angelico.

Maidenhead. SIR THOMAS MERTON: Mainardi, Pseudo Pier Francesco Fiorentino.

Mainz. GALERIE: Lorenzo di Credi.

Malines. MUSÉE COMMUNAL: Daddi.

Manchester. CITY ART GALLERY: Ridolfo Ghirlandajo.

Manhasset (L.I.). MRS. NICHOLAS F. BRADY: Lorenzo di Credi.

Marseille. MUSÉE DES BEAUX-ARTS: Bicci di Lorenzo, Sellajo.

Melbourne. NATIONAL GALLERY OF VICTORIA: Unidentified Florentine 1420–1465.

Melbourne Hall (Derbyshire). LADY KERR: Alunno di Benozzo.

Melun. MUSÉE MUNICIPAL: Pseudo Pier Francesco Fiorentino.

Memphis (Tennessee). BROOKS MEMORIAL ART GALLERY: Bachiacca, Giotto Follower, Giovanni del Biondo, Filippino Lippi, Sellajo, 'Tommaso', Unidentified Florentine 1465–1540.

Mestre (Venice). CASARIN COLLECTION: Bachiacca.

Milan. PINACOTECA AMBROSIANA: Botticelli, Bugiardini, Leonardo da Vinci.

PINACOTECA DI BRERA: Bronzino, Gozzoli.

MUSEI CIVICI DEL CASTELLO SFORZESCO: Leonardo da Vinci, Filippo Lippi, Michelangelo, Pontormo.

MUSEO POLDI PEZZOLI: Albertinelli, Botticelli, Daddi, Domenico Ghirlandajo, Filippo Lippi, Pesellino, Pollajuolo, Raffaellino del Garbo, 'Tommaso', 'Utili'.

DUOMO: Unidentified Florentine 1420–1465.

S. MARIA DELLE GRAZIE: Bugiardini, Leonardo da Vinci.

BARONE ANREP: Daddi.

BRIZIO COLLECTION: Giovanni di Francesco.

CHIESA COLLECTION (EX): Francesco di Antonio.

CRESPI COLLECTION (EX): Lorenzo Monaco.

COMM. ALDO CRESPI: Daddi.

COMM. MARIO CRESPI: Botticelli, Domenico di Michelino.

GIULIO FERRARIO: Puligo.

DUCA GALLARATI SCOTTI: Piero di Cosimo.

COMM. PAOLO GERLI: Fra Diamante.

CONTESSA RASINI: Filippino Lippi, Sellajo.

Minneapolis. INSTITUTE OF ARTS: Daddi, Ridolfo Ghirlandajo, Machiavelli, Master of S. Miniato, Paolo Schiavo, Rosselli.

Modena. GALLERIA ESTENSE: Apollonio di Giovanni, Botticini, Bugiardini, Lorenzo di Credi, Fra Paolino, Puligo, Sogliani, 'Tommaso'.

Montauban. MUSÉE INGRES: Andrea di Giusto, Masolino, 'Utili'.

Montecarlo (Valdarno Superiore). S. FRANCESCO: Fra Angelico, Neri di Bicci.

Montecastello (Pontedera). CANONICA: Andrea di Giusto.

Montefalco. PINACOTECA COMUNALE (S. FRANCESCO): Alunno di Benozzo, Gozzoli.
  S. FORTUNATO: Gozzoli.

Montefioralle (Chianti). PIEVE: Master of S. Miniato.

Montefortino (Amandola). PINACOTECA CIVICA: Botticini, Pier Francesco Fiorentino.

Montelupo (Firenze). S. GIOVANNI: Botticelli.

Montemarciano (Valdarno Superiore). MADONNA DELLE GRAZIE: Masaccio.

Montemurlo (Prato). PIEVE DI S. GIOVANNI BATTISTA: Granacci.

Montepulciano. MUSEO CIVICO: Bicci di Lorenzo, Filippino Lippi, Raffaellino del Garbo, Spinello Aretino.
  S. AGOSTINO: Lorenzo di Credi.

Monterinaldi (Chianti): PARROCCHIALE: Daddi.

Monte San Savino. S. MARIA DELLE VERTIGHE: Lorenzo Monaco.

Montgomery (Alabama). MUSEUM OF ART: Francesco di Antonio.
  HUNTINGDON COLLEGE: Unidentified Florentine 1350–1420.

Montpellier. MUSÉE FABRE: Botticelli, Giovanni di Francesco, Puligo, 'Tommaso'.

Montreal. MUSEUM OF FINE ARTS: Botticelli, Botticini, Domenico di Michelino, Giovanni del Biondo, Granacci, Niccolò di Pietro Gerini.
  R. W. REFORD: Bronzino.

Morrocco (Tavarnelle, Val di Pesa). S. MARIA: Giovanni di Francesco, Neri di Bicci.

Mosciano (Florence). PARISH CHURCH: Cimabue.

Moscow. PUSHKIN MUSEUM: Botticelli, Bronzino, Cristiani, Lorenzo Monaco, Rossello di Jacopo.

Moulins. MUSÉE: Neri di Bicci.

Mount Browne (Guildford, Surrey). LADY ISABEL PEYRONNET BROWNE (EX): Niccolò di Pietro Gerini.

Mühlheim (Cologne). DR. F. THYSSEN (EX): Mainardi.

Muncie (Indiana). BALL STATE TEACHERS COLLEGE: Andrea del Sarto, Giovanni del Biondo, Lorenzo di Credi, Puligo.

Munich. BAYERISCHE STAATSGEMÄLDESAMMLUNGEN (ALTE PINAKOTHEK): Albertinelli, Andrea del Sarto, Fra Angelico, Bachiacca, Botticelli, Daddi, Franciabigio, Agnolo Gaddi, Taddeo Gaddi, Domenico Ghirlandajo, Giotto Assistant, Giusto d'Andrea, Granacci, Leonardo da Vinci, Filippino Lippi, Filippo Lippi, Lorenzo di Niccolò, Mainardi, Masolino, Master of the Bambino Vispo, Master of the Castello Nativity, Nardo di Cione, Niccolò di Pietro Gerini, Piero di Cosimo, Pontormo, Raffaellino del Garbo, Sellajo, 'Tommaso', 'Utili'.
  MARCZELL VON NEMES (EX): Master of the Castello Nativity.
  ERWIN ROSENTHAL (EX): Davide Ghirlandajo, Mariotto di Nardo.

Münster. SEMINAR: Domenico Veneziano, Leonardo da Pistoia, Lorenzo Monaco.

Naarden (Holland). DR. R. WETZLAR: Master of S. Miniato.

Nancy. MUSÉE DES BEAUX-ARTS: Filippino Lippi, Pseudo Pier Francesco Fiorentino, Sogliani.

Nantes. MUSÉE DES BEAUX-ARTS: Bicci di Lorenzo, Daddi, Mariotto di Nardo, Neri di Bicci, Puligo, Sellajo.

Naples. GALLERIA NAZIONALE (CAPODIMONTE): Andrea del Sarto, Fra Bartolommeo, Botticelli, Daddi, Filippino Lippi, Lorenzo di Credi, Mainardi, Masaccio, Masolino, Raffaellino del Garbo, Rosso Fiorentino.

    MUSEO FILANGERI: Botticelli.

    MUSEO DI S. MARTINO: Niccolò di Tommaso.

    CASTELNUOVO: Maso di Banco.

    S. CHIARA: Giotto Follower.

    S. MARIA DEL POPOLO (OSPEDALE DEGLI INCURABILI): Bugiardini.

    DUCA DI MONTALTINO (EX): Puligo.

Narbonne. MUSÉE D'ART ET D'HISTOIRE: Andrea di Giusto, Pseudo Pier Francesco Fiorentino.

Narni. PINACOTECA. Bartolomeo di Giovanni, Domenico Ghirlandajo, Gozzoli.

Nashville (Tennessee). G. PEABODY COLLEGE: Unidentified Florentine 1350–1420.

Nevers. MUSÉE: Mariotto di Nardo.

Neviges (Rheinland). FRAU F. SCHNIEWIND: Fra Angelico.

New Haven (Conn.). YALE UNIVERSITY ART GALLERY: Apollonio di Giovanni, Bartolomeo di Giovanni, Botticelli, Bugiardini, Cristiani, Daddi, Domenico di Michelino, Agnolo Gaddi, Taddeo Gaddi, Domenico Ghirlandajo, Ridolfo Ghirlandajo, Giovanni del Biondo, Giovanni dal Ponte, Granacci, Jacopo del Casentino, Jacopo di Cione, Leonardo da Pistoia, Filippino Lippi, Lorenzo di Credi, Lorenzo Monaco, Lorenzo di Niccolò, Machiavelli, Mariotto di Nardo, Master of the Bambino Vispo, Master of the Castello Nativity, Master of S. Miniato, Nardo di Cione, Neri di Bicci, Niccolò di Pietro Gerini, Niccolò di Tommaso, Paolo Schiavo, Pesellino, Pseudo Pier Francesco Fiorentino, Piero di Cosimo, Pollajuolo, Puligo, Rossello di Jacopo, Sellajo, Sogliani, 'Tommaso', 'Utili', Unidentified Florentine 1350–1420, Unidentified Florentine 1420–1465.

New Orleans. ISAAC DELGADO MUSEUM OF ART: Bachiacca, Bugiardini, Daddi, Giovanni del Biondo, Filippo Lippi.

New York. METROPOLITAN MUSEUM OF ART: Andrea del Sarto, Fra Angelico, Bachiacca, Baldovinetti, Bartolomeo di Giovanni, Bicci di Lorenzo, Botticelli, Bronzino, Bugiardini, Castagno, Cristiani, Daddi, Domenico Veneziano, Franciabigio, Agnolo Gaddi, Taddeo Gaddi, Domenico Ghirlandajo, Ridolfo Ghirlandajo, Giotto Assistant, Giovanni da Milano, Gozzoli, Jacopo di Cione, Filippino Lippi, Filippo Lippi, Lorenzo di Credi, Lorenzo Monaco, Lorenzo di Niccolò, Mainardi, Mariotto di Nardo, Maso di Banco, Master of the Barberini Panels, Pesellino, Pseudo Pier Francesco Fiorentino, Piero di Cosimo, Pollajuolo, Rosselli, Rossello di Jacopo, Sellajo, Spinello Aretino, Tommaso di Stefano Lunetti, 'Utili', Verrocchio, Unidentified Florentine 1350–1420, Unidentified Florentine 1420–1465.

    FRICK COLLECTION: Bronzino, Castagno, Cimabue, Filippo Lippi.

    GUGGENHEIM MUSEUM: Lorenzo Monaco.

    HISTORICAL SOCIETY: Daddi, Domenico Veneziano, Francesco di Antonio, Taddeo Gaddi, Filippino Lippi, Mariotto di Nardo, Nardo di Cione, Neri di Bicci, Pesellino,

Northampton (Mass.). SMITH COLLEGE: Jacopo di Cione.

North Mimms (Herts.). MRS. WALTER BURNS: Daddi, Rosselli.

Northwick Park (Blockley). CAPT. E. G. SPENCER CHURCHILL: Fra Angelico, Rosselli.

Norton Hall (Glos.). SIR WALTER AND LADY POLLEN: Fra Bartolommeo, Davide Ghirlandajo, Puligo.

Notre Dame (Ind.). UNIVERSITY: Andrea da Firenze, Baldovinetti, Fra Paolino, Rosselli.

Nottingham. ST. MARY'S: Fra Bartolommeo.

Novoli (Firenze). S. MARIA (EX): Masolino.

Oakly Park (Shrops.). EARL OF PLYMOUTH: Giovanni dal Ponte, Piero di Cosimo, Puligo.

Oberlin (Ohio). ALLEN MEMORIAL ART MUSEUM: Apollonio di Giovanni, Mariotto di Nardo.
  COLLEGE: Neri di Bicci.

Olantigh Towers (Wye Kent). MR. SAWBRIDGE-ERLE-DRAX (EX): Raffaellino del Garbo.

Omaha (Nebraska). JOSLYN MEMORIAL ART MUSEUM: Jacopo di Cione, Lorenzo di Credi.

Orléans. MUSÉE DES BEAUX-ARTS: Fra Paolino, Raffaellino del Garbo.

Ortimino (Val d'Elsa). S. VITO: Rossello di Jacopo.

Orvieto. DUOMO: Fra Angelico, Botticelli, Gozzoli.

Ottawa. NATIONAL GALLERY OF CANADA: Botticelli, Bronzino, Giotto Follower, Gozzoli, Filippino Lippi, Lippo di Benivieni, Neri di Bicci, Piero di Cosimo, Puligo, Unidentified Florentine 1350–1420.

Oxford. ASHMOLEAN MUSEUM: Fra Angelico, Apollonio di Giovanni, Bicci di Lorenzo, Bronzino, Daddi, Franciabigio, Davide Ghirlandajo, Giotto Follower, Giovanni di Francesco, Granacci, Filippo Lippi, Lorenzo di Credi, Orcagna, Piero di Cosimo, Raffaellino del Garbo, Rosselli, Uccello, 'Utili'.
  CHRIST CHURCH LIBRARY: Bachiacca, Bartolomeo di Giovanni, Granacci, Filippino Lippi, Lorenzo di Niccolò, Mariotto di Nardo, Master of the Bambino Vispo, Master of S. Cecilia, Neri di Bicci, Niccolò di Pietro Gerini, Orcagna, Piero di Cosimo, Pontormo, Raffaellino del Garbo, Sellajo, Spinello Aretino, 'Utili', Unidentified Florentine 1420–1465.
  CAMPION HALL: Master of S. Miniato.

Padua. MUSEO CIVICO: Giotto.
  S. ANTONIO: Giotto Assistant.
  ARENA CHAPEL: Giotto.

Pagiano (Valdarno Superiore). S. MARTINO: Granacci.

Palermo. GALLERIA NAZIONALE: Lorenzo di Credi, Sogliani.
  S. NICCOLÒ REALE (MUSEO DIOCESANO): Antonio Veneziano.
  CHIARAMONTE BORDONARO COLLECTION: Bartolomeo di Giovanni, Botticelli, Mainardi, Mariotto di Nardo, Neri di Bicci, Pseudo Pier Francesco Fiorentino, Sellajo.

Panzano. PIEVE DI S. LEONINO: Mariotto di Nardo.
  S. MARIA: Botticini, Michele di Ridolfo.

Paray-le-Monial. MUSÉE MUNICIPAL: Neri di Bicci.

Parcieux. GEORGES CHALANDON: Bartolomeo di Giovanni.
  HENRI CHALANDON (EX): Lorenzo Monaco, Mariotto di Nardo.

Paris. MUSÉES NATIONAUX: Albertinelli, Alunno di Benozzo, Andrea di Giusto, Botticelli, Francesco di Antonio, Taddeo Gaddi, Mariotto di Nardo, Master of S. Miniato,

Michele di Ridolfo, Niccolò di Pietro Gerini, Niccolò di Tommaso, Pier Francesco Fiorentino, Pseudo Pier Francesco Fiorentino, Sellajo, Sogliani, 'Utili', Unidentified Florentine 1350–1420.

MUSÉE DU LOUVRE: Albertinelli, Andrea di Giusto, Andrea del Sarto, Fra Angelico, Baldovinetti, Fra Bartolommeo, Bartolomeo di Giovanni, Botticelli, Botticini, Bronzino, Cimabue, Daddi, Fra Diamante, Domenico di Michelino, Franciabigio, Agnolo Gaddi, Domenico Ghirlandajo, Ridolfo Ghirlandajo, Giotto Assistant, Giotto Follower, Giovanni dal Ponte, Gozzoli, Leonardo di Vinci, Filippino Lippi, Filippo Lippi, Lorenzo di Credi, Lorenzo Monaco, Mainardi, Mariotto di Nardo, Master of the Arte della Lana Coronation, Master of the Castello Nativity, Michelangelo, Neri di Bicci, Niccolò di Pietro Gerini, Pesellino, Pseudo Pier Francesco Fiorentino, Piero di Cosimo, Pontormo, Puligo, Raffaellino del Garbo, Rosselli, Rosso Fiorentino, Sellajo, Uccello, 'Utili', Verrocchio.

MUSÉE JACQUEMART-ANDRÉ: Baldovinetti, Botticelli, Botticini, Bugiardini, Domenico di Michelino, Giovanni dal Ponte, Neri di Bicci, Pseudo Pier Francesco Fiorentino, Pontormo, Uccello, 'Utili'.

MUSÉE DE CLUNY: Apollonio di Giovanni, Botticini, Davide Ghirlandajo, Master of the Bambino Vispo, Rossello di Jacopo.

MUSÉE DES ARTS DÉCORATIFS: Bugiardini, Daddi, Mariotto di Nardo, Rosselli, 'Utili'.

BIBLIOTHÈQUE NATIONALE: Francesco di Antonio.

ÉCOLE DES BEAUX-ARTS: Spinello Aretino.

BARON CASSEL (EX): Giovanni dal Ponte.

LUCIEN COTTREAU (EX): Bugiardini.

PAUL DELAROFF (EX): Alunno di Benozzo.

JEAN DOLLFUS (EX): Master of S. Miniato.

GUSTAVE DREYFUS (EX): Mainardi.

LOUIS FOURNIER (EX): Leonardo da Pistoia.

DUC DE GRAMMONT (EX?): Bugiardini.

HEUGEL COLLECTION (EX): Botticini, Filippino Lippi, Neri di Bicci.

MARTIN LE ROY (EX): Giovanni da Milano.

ARTAUD DE MONTOR (EX): Cimabue.

CHARLES PERRIOLAT (EX): Andrea di Giusto, Neri di Bicci.

COMTE DE POURTALÈS (EX): Albertinelli.

E. RICHTEMBERGER (EX): Raffaellino del Garbo, Unidentified Florentine 1465–1540.

BARONNE ÉDOUARD DE ROTHSCHILD: Raffaellino del Garbo.

ROUART COLLECTION (EX): Agnolo Gaddi.

MME. DE RUBLÉ: Leonardo da Vinci.

JOSEPH SPIRIDON (EX): Lorenzo Monaco.

COMTESSE DE VOGÜÉ: Filippino Lippi.

Parma. GALLERIA NAZIONALE: Fra Angelico, Bicci di Lorenzo, Botticelli, Daddi, Agnolo Gaddi, Giusto d'Andrea, Lorenzo di Niccolò, Master of the Bambino Vispo, Neri di Bicci, Niccolò di Pietro Gerini, Spinello Aretino.

CONGREGAZIONE DI S. FILIPPO NERI (PINACOTECA STUARD): Bicci di Lorenzo, Giovanni di Francesco, Niccolò di Tommaso.

Passignano (Val di Pesa). BADIA: Domenico Ghirlandajo, Michele di Ridolfo.

Pavia. MUSEO MALASPINA: Jacopo del Casentino, Master of S. Miniato, Sellajo, Spinello.

Pelago (Firenze). ORATORIO DEL MAGNALE: Lorenzo di Niccolò.

S. MARTINO A PAGIANO: Lorenzo di Niccolò.

PIEVE DI RISTONCHI: Unidentified Florentine 1420–1465.

Périgueux. MUSÉE DU PÉRIGORD: Botticelli, 'Utili'.

Perpignan. MUSÉE RIGAUD: Pier Francesco Fiorentino.

Perugia. GALLERIA NAZIONALE DELL'UMBRIA: Fra Angelico, Bicci di Lorenzo, Gozzoli, Piero di Cosimo.

DUOMO, MUSEO DELL'OPERA: Agnolo Gaddi.

S. DOMENICO: Mariotto di Nardo.

R. VAN MARLE (EX): Bicci di Lorenzo, Giovanni dal Ponte, Neri di Bicci.

Pesaro. MUSEO CIVICO: Mariotto di Nardo.

Pescia. MUSEO (BIBLIOTECA COMUNALE): Lorenzo Monaco, Lorenzo di Niccolò, Master of S. Cecilia, Neri di Bicci.

BIBLIOTECA CAPITOLARE: Bicci di Lorenzo.

S. ANTONIO ABATE: Bicci di Lorenzo.

S. FRANCESCO: Bicci di Lorenzo, Neri di Bicci.

Petrognano (Val d'Elsa). S. PIETRO: Unidentified Florentine 1350–1420.

Petworth House (Sussex). NATIONAL TRUST: Andrea del Sarto.

Philadelphia (Pa.). MUSEUM OF ART: Bartolomeo di Giovanni, Bronzino, Master of the Bambino Vispo.

— JOHN G. JOHNSON COLLECTION: Albertinelli, Andrea di Giusto, Andrea del Sarto, Fra Angelico, Bachiacca, Fra Bartolommeo, Bartolomeo di Giovanni, Botticelli, Daddi, Domenico di Michelino, Benedetto Ghirlandajo, Davide Ghirlandajo, Domenico Ghirlandajo, Ridolfo Ghirlandajo, Giotto Follower, Giovanni del Biondo, Giovanni di Francesco, Giovanni dal Ponte, Gozzoli, Jacopo di Cione, Leonardo da Pistoia, Lorenzo di Credi, Lorenzo Monaco, Mainardi, Masolino, Master of the Bambino Vispo, Master of the Castello Nativity, Master of S. Miniato, Neri di Bicci, Niccolò di Pietro Gerini, Niccolò di Tommaso, Pesellino, Pseudo Pier Francesco Fiorentino, Piero di Cosimo, Pontormo, Puligo, Rosselli, Sellajo, 'Utili', Unidentified Florentine 1420–1465.

— W. P. WILSTACH COLLECTION (EX): Neri di Bicci.

ACADEMY OF FINE ARTS: Pseudo Pier Francesco Fiorentino.

JOHN D. MCILHENNY (EX): Master of the Bambino Vispo, Master of S. Miniato.

Piacenza. MUSEO CIVICO: Botticelli.

Pisa. MUSEO NAZIONALE DI S. MATTEO: Alunno di Benozzo, Fra Angelico, Bicci di Lorenzo, Daddi, Fra Diamante, Francesco di Antonio, Davide Ghirlandajo, Domenico Ghirlandajo, Giovanni del Biondo, Giovanni dal Ponte, Giusto d'Andrea, Gozzoli, Lorenzo Monaco, Lorenzo di Niccolò, Machiavelli, Mainardi, Masaccio, Master of the Bambino Vispo, Master of the Castello Nativity, Neri di Bicci, Niccolò di Tommaso, Paolo Schiavo, Puligo, Raffaellino del Garbo, Rossello di Jacopo, Rosso Fiorentino, Sogliani, Spinello Aretino, Unidentified Florentine 1420–1465.

ARCIVESCOVADO: Gozzoli.

CAMPOSANTO: Andrea da Firenze, Antonio Veneziano, Taddeo Gaddi, Gozzoli, Spinello Aretino.

DUOMO: Andrea del Sarto, Cimabue, Lorenzo di Niccolò, Sogliani, Spinello Aretino.

S. CATERINA: Fra Bartolommeo.

Prato (*contd.*) DUOMO: Andrea di Giusto, Fra Diamante, Agnolo Gaddi, Ridolfo Ghirlandajo, Giovanni di Francesco, Filippo Lippi, Pietro di Miniato.

S. FRANCESCO: Niccolò di Pietro Gerini.

S. NICOLA: Giovanni da Milano.

S. SPIRITO: Fra Diamante, Filippo Lippi, Sogliani.

CONVENTO DI S. MATTEO: Pietro di Miniato.

Princeton (N.J.). UNIVERSITY ART MUSEUM: Alunno di Benozzo, Fra Angelico, Domenico Ghirlandajo, Giovanni del Biondo, Mariotto di Nardo, Sellajo, 'Utili', Unidentified Florentine 1465–1540.

MRS. DOUGLAS DELANOY: Jacopo del Casentino.

Providence (R.I.). RHODE ISLAND SCHOOL OF DESIGN: Domenico di Michelino (ex), Jacopo di Cione, Mariotto di Nardo, Spinello Aretino.

Radda (Chianti). PALAZZO COMUNALE: Davide Ghirlandajo.

Radensleben. W. VON QUAST (EX): Daddi, Jacopo di Cione.

Radicondoli (Siena). S. SIMONE: Master of the Bambino Vispo.

Raleigh (North Carolina). MUSEUM OF ART: Andrea del Sarto, Apollonio di Giovanni, Botticelli, Filippino Lippi, Lorenzo di Niccolò, Maso di Banco, Master of the Rinuccini Chapel, Unidentified Florentine 1350–1420.

Ravenna. ACCADEMIA: Lorenzo Monaco, 'Utili'.

Reggello (Valdarno Superiore). S. PIETRO A PITIANA: Ridolfo Ghirlandajo.

Reigate Priory (Surrey). LADY HENRY SOMERSET (EX): Granacci.

Rennes. MUSÉE DES BEAUX-ARTS: Andrea di Giusto, Lorenzo di Niccolò.

Richmond (Surrey). COOK COLLECTION: Fra Bartolommeo, Filippo Lippi.

— (EX): Andrea del Sarto, Bachiacca, Bartolomeo di Giovanni, Botticelli, Botticini, Giovanni del Biondo, Pseudo Pier Francesco Fiorentino.

Rignano sull' Arno (Miransù). S. LORENZO: Neri di Bicci.

Rimini. PINACOTECA COMUNALE: Domenico Ghirlandajo.

S. FRANCESCO: Giotto.

Rochester (N.Y.): MEMORIAL ART GALLERY: Bachiacca.

Rome. GALLERIA NAZIONALE (PALAZZO BARBERINI): Andrea del Sarto, Fra Angelico, Fra Bartolommeo, Bronzino, Franciabigio, Giovanni da Milano, Filippo Lippi, Michelangelo Follower, Orcagna, Fra Paolino, Piero di Cosimo, Pontormo, Rosselli, Tommaso di Stefano Lunetti.

GALLERIA NAZIONALE (PALAZZO CORSINI): Jacopo del Casentino.

GALLERIA BORGHESE: Albertinelli, Andrea del Sarto, Bachiacca, Botticelli, Bronzino, Franciabigio, Granacci, Lorenzo di Credi, Michele di Ridolfo, Piero di Cosimo, Pontormo, Puligo, 'Tommaso', Unidentified Florentine 1465–1540.

GALLERIA COLONNA: Bartolomeo di Giovanni, Botticelli, Bronzino, Bugiardini, Franciabigio, Michele di Ridolfo, Puligo, Sellajo.

GALLERIA DORIA PAMPHILJ: Andrea del Sarto, Bicci di Lorenzo, Bronzino, Filippo Lippi, Master of the Bambino Vispo, Fra Paolino, Pesellino.

MUSEO DEL CASTEL S. ANGELO: Taddeo Gaddi.

ACCADEMIA DI SAN LUCA: Master of S. Miniato.

MUSEO DI PALAZZO VENEZIA: Bachiacca, Bugiardini, Gozzoli, Jacopo di Cione, Master of the Bambino Vispo, Puligo, Unidentified Florentine 1465–1540.

Rome (*contd.*) MARCHESA VISCONTI VENOSTA: Fra Bartolommeo, Daddi, Master of the Bambino Vispo.

Romena (Casentino). PIEVE DI S. PIETRO: Giovanni del Biondo, Unidentified Florentine 1465–1540.

Rosano (Pontassieve). SS. ANNUNZIATA: Giovanni dal Ponte.

PARROCCHIALE: Jacopo di Cione.

Rossie Priory (Inchture, Perthshire). LORD KINNAIRD (EX): Granacci.

Rotterdam. MUSEUM BOYMANS—VAN BEUNINGEN: Bachiacca, Davide Ghirlandajo, Jacopo di Cione, Master of the Bambino Vispo, Master of S. Miniato, Neri di Bicci, Sellajo, Spinello Aretino.

Rouen. MUSÉE DES BEAUX-ARTS: Master of the Arte della Lana Coronation, Neri di Bicci.

Saint Louis (Missouri). CITY ART MUSEUM: Davide Ghirlandajo, Jacopo di Cione, Lorenzo di Niccolò, Piero di Cosimo, Spinello Aretino.

Salisbury (Wilts.). JULIAN SALMOND: Puligo.

San Antonio (Texas). WITTE MEMORIAL MUSEUM: Unidentified Florentine 1465–1540.

San Casciano (Val di Pesa). S. FRANCESCO: 'Utili'.

S. GIOVANNI IN SUGANA: Neri di Bicci.

San Diego (Cal.). FINE ARTS GALLERY: Giotto Assistant, Lorenzo Monaco, Neri di Bicci, Piero di Cosimo.

San Donato in Poggio (Val di Pesa). PIEVE: Bicci di Lorenzo, Giovanni del Biondo.

Sands Point (L.I.). MRS. HANNAH RABINOWITZ: Master of the Castello Nativity.

San Francisco (Cal.). M. H. DE YOUNG MEMORIAL MUSEUM: Fra Angelico, Antonio Veneziano, Bartolomeo di Giovanni, Bicci di Lorenzo, Bronzino, Daddi, Giovanni dal Ponte, Granacci, Jacopo di Cione, Pontormo, Raffaellino del Garbo, Unidentified Florentine 1420–1465.

San Gimignano. MUSEO CIVICO: Giusto d'Andrea, Gozzoli, Filippino Lippi, Lorenzo di Niccolò, Mainardi, Neri di Bicci, Pier Francesco Fiorentino, Unidentified Florentine 1420–1465, Unidentified Florentine 1465–1540.

VIA S. GIOVANNI: Mainardi.

COLLEGIATA: Domenico Ghirlandajo, Gozzoli, Mainardi, Michele di Ridolfo, Pier Francesco Fiorentino.

S. AGOSTINO: Gozzoli, Mainardi, Fra Paolino, Pier Francesco Fiorentino, Pollajuolo.

S. JACOPO: Pier Francesco Fiorentino.

S. LUCIA: Fra Paolino, Pier Francesco Fiorentino.

S. MARIA ASSUNTA A PANCOLE: Pier Francesco Fiorentino.

OSPEDALE DI S. FINA: Mainardi.

(Environs). CONVENTO DI MONTE OLIVETO: Gozzoli.

Sanginesio (Macerata). PINACOTECA: Domenico Ghirlandajo.

San Giovanni Valdarno. MUSEO: Francesco di Antonio, Giovanni del Biondo, Giusto d'Andrea, Sellajo, Unidentified Florentine 1420–1465.

PIEVE DI S. GIOVANNI BATTISTA: Jacopo di Cione.

CONSERVATORIO DELLE AGOSTINIANE: Master of the Castello Nativity.

San Godenzo (Mugello). BADIA: Daddi, Sogliani.

San Marino (Cal.). HUNTINGTON MUSEUM: Lorenzo di Credi, Mainardi, Master of the Castello Nativity, Michele di Ridolfo, Pseudo Pier Francesco Fiorentino, Rosselli.

San Miniato al Tedesco (Pisa). PALAZZO COMUNALE: Cenni di Francesco.

   s. DOMENICO: Cenni di Francesco, Giovanni del Biondo, Giusto d'Andrea, Mariotto di Nardo, Master of S. Miniato, Paolo Schiavo, Rossello di Jacopo.

   MISERICORDIA: Master of S. Miniato.

   ORATORIO DEL LORETINO: Puligo.

San Piero a Sieve (Mugello). TABERNACOLO DELLE MOZZETTE: Paolo Schiavo.

Sant' Agata (Scarperia, Mugello). PIEVE: Bicci di Lorenzo, Giovanni del Biondo, Rossello di Jacopo.

Santa Barbara (Cal.). MUSEUM OF ART: Agnolo Gaddi.

   UNIVERSITY OF CALIFORNIA: Granacci, Pseudo Pier Francesco Fiorentino.

   MRS. GEORGE F. STEEDMAN: Mariotto di Nardo.

Santa Monica (Cal.). J. PAUL GETTY MUSEUM: 'Tommaso'.

San Vivaldo (Gambassi, Val d'Elsa). s. MARIA IN CAMPORENA: Raffaellino del Garbo.

São Paulo (Brazil). MUSEU DE ARTE: Daddi, Pseudo Pier Francesco Fiorentino, Piero di Cosimo, 'Utili'.

Sarasota (Florida). JOHN AND MABLE RINGLING MUSEUM OF ART: Albertinelli, Fra Bartolommeo, Giovanni del Biondo, Granacci, Mainardi, Mariotto di Nardo, Master of the Lathrop Tondo, Paolo Schiavo, Piero di Cosimo, Puligo, Raffaellino del Garbo, Sellajo.

Scarperia (Mugello). MADONNA DELLE GRAZIE: Jacopo del Casentino, Unidentified Florentine 1420–1465.

Seattle (Washington). ART MUSEUM: Fra Bartolommeo, Daddi, Francesco di Antonio, Lorenzo Monaco, 'Tommaso', Unidentified Florentine 1420–1465, Unidentified Florentine 1465–1540.

   UNIVERSITY OF WASHINGTON, HENRY ART GALLERY: Unidentified Florentine 1465–1540.

Seebenstein (Austria). LIECHTENSTEIN COLLECTION (EX): Pesellino.

Sens (Yonne). MUSÉE MUNICIPAL: Master of S. Miniato.

Sermoneta (Lazio). s. MARIA ASSUNTA: Gozzoli.

Serravalle (Pistoia). s. MICHELE: Bocchi.

Settimo (Pisa). s. BENEDETTO: Pontormo.

Seville. MUSEO: Puligo.

   CASA DE LAS DUENAS: Neri di Bicci.

Sheffield. RUSKIN MUSEUM: Verrocchio.

   REV. A. HAWKINS JONES (EX): Fra Angelico.

Shenfield Mill (Berks.). DR. JAMES HASSON: Lorenzo di Credi.

Sherborn (Mass.). MRS. CARL PICKHARDT: Daddi.

Siena. PINACOTECA: Albertinelli, Alunno di Benozzo, Antonio Veneziano, Daddi, Giovanni del Biondo, Lorenzo Monaco, Mariotto di Nardo, Neri di Bicci, Pier Francesco Fiorentino, Rossello di Jacopo, Rosso Fiorentino, Spinello Aretino, Unidentified Florentine 1420–1465.

   PALAZZO PUBBLICO: Spinello Aretino.

   DUOMO: Mainardi.

   s. MARIA DEGLI ANGELI: Raffaellino del Garbo.

   s. SPIRITO: Fra Paolino.

   SARACINI COLLECTION: Mariotto di Nardo.

Sinalunga (Val di Chiana). S. MARTINO: Pseudo Pier Francesco Fiorentino.

Spoleto. DUOMO: Fra Diamante, Filippo Lippi.

Springfield (Mass.). ART MUSEUM: Bachiacca.

Staggia (Poggibonsi). S. MARIA ASSUNTA: Pollajuolo, Raffaellino del Garbo.

—— (EX): Rossello di Jacopo.

Staten Island (N.Y.). INSTITUTE OF ARTS AND SCIENCES: Jacopo del Casentino.

Stia (Casentino). PROPOSITURA (S. MARIA ASSUNTA): Bicci di Lorenzo, Master of the Bambino Vispo.

(Environs). S. LORENZO A PORCIANO: Andrea di Giusto.

— S. MARIA DELLE GRAZIE: Davide Ghirlandajo, Lorenzo di Niccolò, Paolo Schiavo.

Stockholm. NATIONAL MUSEUM: Bronzino, Masolino, Master of the Bambino Vispo, Nardo di Cione, Piero di Cosimo, Sellajo.

ROYAL PALACE: Botticini, Piero di Cosimo.

UNIVERSITY: Bugiardini.

G. STENMAN: Puligo.

Stockton (Cal.). SAN JOAQUIN PIONEER MUSEUM AND HAGGIN MEMORIAL ART GALLERIES: Ridolfo Ghirlandajo.

Strasbourg. MUSÉE DES BEAUX-ARTS: Botticelli, Bronzino, Daddi, Domenico di Michelino, Francesco di Antonio, Taddeo Gaddi, Giotto Assistant, Giovanni dal Ponte, Filippino Lippi, Lorenzo di Credi, Niccolò di Pietro Gerini, Piero di Cosimo, Pollajuolo, 'Utili'.

Stuttgart. STAATSGALERIE: Fra Bartolommeo.

Subiaco. SACRO SPECO: Master of the Bambino Vispo.

Sutton Place (Surrey). DUKE OF SUTHERLAND (EX): Giovanni da Milano.

Tavarnelle (Val di Pesa). S. LUCIA AL BORGHETTO: Neri di Bicci.

Tempe (Arizona). STATE UNIVERSITY: Bicci di Lorenzo.

Templecombe (Somerset). LADY THEODORA GUEST: Michele di Ridolfo.

Terni. PINACOTECA: Gozzoli.

Tewin Water (Welwyn, Herts.). SIR OTTO BEIT (EX): Raffaellino del Garbo.

Todi. PINACOTECA CIVICA: Bicci di Lorenzo, Pseudo Pier Francesco Fiorentino.

S. FORTUNATO: Masolino.

Toledo. CATEDRAL: Antonio Veneziano.

Toledo (Ohio). MUSEUM OF ART: Bronzino, Lorenzo Monaco, Pesellino, Piero di Cosimo, Unidentified Florentine 1465–1540.

JOHN N. WILLYS (EX): Raffaellino del Garbo.

Topsfield (Mass.). MRS. EDWARD JACKSON HOLMES: Rosselli.

Toulon. MUSÉE D'ART: Master of S. Miniato, Puligo, Sogliani.

Toulouse. MUSÉE DES AUGUSTINS: Albertinelli, Filippino Lippi, Neri di Bicci, Sellajo.

Troyes. MUSÉE DES BEAUX-ARTS: Bachiacca.

Tucson (Arizona). UNIVERSITY OF ARIZONA: Domenico di Michelino, Agnolo Gaddi, Jacopo del Casentino.

ST. PHILIP'S IN THE HILLS: Francesco di Antonio, Jacopo di Cione.

Tulsa (Oklahoma). PHILBROOK ART CENTER: Alunno di Benozzo, Andrea di Giusto, Lorenzo Monaco, Pseudo Pier Francesco Fiorentino, Rosselli, Tommaso di Stefano Lunetti, 'Utili'.

Turin. GALLERIA SABAUDA: Fra Angelico, Apollonio di Giovanni, Botticelli, Botticini, Bugiardini, Cimabue, Daddi, Franciabigio, Giovanni da Milano, Filippino Lippi, Lorenzo di Credi, Niccolò di Tommaso, Pollajuolo, Pontormo, Rosselli, Sogliani, Unidentified Florentine 1420–1465.

MUSEO CIVICO (PALAZZO MADAMA): Albertinelli, Bugiardini, Daddi, Lorenzo Monaco.

ACCADEMIA ALBERTINA: Filippo Lippi.

ARMERIA REALE: Rosso Fiorentino.

GUALINO COLLECTION (EX): Andrea di Giusto, Botticini.

Tynninghame (Prestonkirk, Haddington, East Lothian). EARL OF HADDINGTON: Michele di Ridolfo.

Udine. MUSEO CIVICO: Albertinelli, Bicci di Lorenzo.

Ulignano (Val d'Elsa). PIEVE: Pier Francesco Fiorentino.

Upton House (Banbury, Oxon.). NATIONAL TRUST: Daddi, Master of S. Miniato, Rosselli.

Urbino. GALLERIA NAZIONALE DELLE MARCHE (PALAZZO DUCALE): Domenico Ghirlandajo, Uccello.

Utrecht. ARCHIEPISCOPAL MUSEUM: Daddi, Mariotto di Nardo, Neri di Bicci, Orcagna.

ART INSTITUTE: Neri di Bicci.

Vaduz. LIECHTENSTEIN COLLECTION: Franciabigio, Agnolo Gaddi, Leonardo da Vinci, Lorenzo di Credi, Lorenzo Monaco, Mainardi, Mariotto di Nardo, Piero di Cosimo, Pontormo, Sellajo, Unidentified Florentine 1465–1540.

Vallombrosa. ABBAZIA: Raffaellino del Garbo.

Varramista (Pisa). PIAGGIO COLLECTION: Pontormo.

Velletri. MUSEO DEL DUOMO: Bicci di Lorenzo.

Venice. GALLERIA DELL'ACCADEMIA: Antonio da Firenze, Raffaellino del Garbo.

MUSEO CIVICO CORRER: Apollonio di Giovanni.

PINACOTECA QUERINI STAMPALIA: Lorenzo di Credi.

BIBLIOTECA MARCIANA: Pesellino.

CA D'ORO: Bicci di Lorenzo, Botticini, Bugiardini, Davide Ghirlandajo, Niccolò di Tommaso, Pseudo Pier Francesco Fiorentino, Sellajo, 'Utili', Unidentified Florentine 1465–1540.

CAMPO SS. GIOVANNI E PAOLO: Verrocchio.

PALAZZO GRASSI: Sellajo.

S. MARCO: Castagno.

S. ZACCARIA: Castagno.

SEMINARIO: Albertinelli, Filippino Lippi, Puligo.

CONTE VITTORIO CINI: Fra Angelico, Daddi, Giovanni dal Ponte, Filippo Lippi, Mainardi, Master of S. Cecilia, Piero di Cosimo, Pontormo, Sellajo.

MARIANO FORTUNY COLLECTION (EX): Taddeo Gaddi.

PRINCIPE GIOVANNELLI (EX): Bachiacca.

Vercelli. MUSEO BORGOGNA: Bartolomeo di Giovanni, Mariotto di Nardo.

Verona. MUSEO DI CASTELVECCHIO: Daddi, Niccolò di Pietro Gerini, Pesellino.

Vertine (Chianti). S. BARTOLOMEO: Bicci di Lorenzo.

Vespignano (Vicchio di Mugello). S. MARTINO: Paolo Schiavo.

Vienna. KUNSTHISTORISCHES MUSEUM: Andrea di Giusto, Andrea del Sarto, Fra Bartolommeo, Bronzino, Bugiardini, Franciabigio, Gozzoli, Machiavelli, Mariotto di Nardo, Pontormo, Rosso Fiorentino.

AKADEMIE: Botticelli, Francesco di Antonio, Michelangelo Follower Fra Paolino, Puligo, Sellajo.

DIÖZESANMUSEUM: Fra Paolino.

AUSPITZ COLLECTION (EX): Cristiani.

OSCAR BONDY (EX): Jacopo del Casentino, Unidentified Florentine 1350–1420.

CZERNIN COLLECTION (EX): Puligo.

DR. HERMANN EISSLER (EX): Alunno di Benozzo, Antonio Veneziano.

HARRACH GALLERY: Mainardi.

LANCKORONSKI COLLECTION: Apollonio di Giovanni (ex), Bartolomeo di Giovanni, Bicci di Lorenzo, Daddi (ex), Fra Diamante, Domenico Veneziano, Mariotto di Nardo, Masaccio, Master of the Castello Nativity, Niccolò di Pietro Gerini, Niccolò di Tommaso, Piero di Cosimo, Rossello di Jacopo, Sellajo, Sogliani, Spinello Aretino, 'Utili'.

LEDERER COLLECTION (EX): Master of the Bambino Vispo.

CARL MOLL (EX): Rossello di Jacopo.

EMIL WEINBERGER (EX): Jacopo del Casentino.

WITTGENSTEIN COLLECTION (EX): 'Tommaso'.

(Environs). OBER ST. VEIT FANITEUM: Neri di Bicci.

Villamagna (Volterra). PIEVE: Rosso Fiorentino.

MADONNA DELLE NEVI: Pier Francesco Fiorentino.

Vinci (Empoli). ORATORIO DELL'ANNUNCIATA: Fra Paolino.

Viterbo. S. MARIA DELLA QUERCE: Fra Paolino.

S. SISTO: Neri di Bicci.

Volognano (Pontassieve). S. MICHELE: Albertinelli.

Volterra. PINACOTECA COMUNALE: Alvaro Portoghese, Bugiardini, Cenni di Francesco, Domenico Ghirlandajo, Jacopo di Cione, Leonardo da Pistoia, Neri di Bicci, Raffaellino del Garbo, Rosso Fiorentino, Sogliani.

PALAZZO DEI PRIORI: Pier Francesco Fiorentino, Raffaellino del Garbo.

DUOMO: Albertinelli, Gozzoli.

S. FRANCESCO: Cenni di Francesco.

S. GIROLAMO: Giusto d'Andrea.

SS. GIUSTO E CLEMENTE: Neri di Bicci.

Warsaw. MUSEUM: Bocchi.

Warwick Castle. EARL OF WARWICK: Granacci, Pontormo.

Washington. (D.C.). NATIONAL GALLERY OF ART: Andrea del Sarto, Fra Angelico, Bachiacca, Botticelli, Bronzino, Castagno, Cimabue, Daddi, Domenico Veneziano, Agnolo Gaddi, Domenico Ghirlandajo, Ridolfo Ghirlandajo, Giotto, Gozzoli, Granacci, Jacopo di Cione, Filippino Lippi, Filippo Lippi, Lorenzo di Credi, Lorenzo Monaco, Masaccio, Masolino, Master of the Barberini Panels, Nardo di Cione, Orcagna, Pesellino, Pseudo Pier Francesco Fiorentino, Piero di Cosimo, Pontormo, Rosso Fiorentino, Sellajo, 'Utili', Verrocchio.

SMITHSONIAN INSTITUTION: Mainardi.

DUMBARTON OAKS: Daddi.

HOWARD UNIVERSITY: Granacci.

West Orange (N.J.). NILS B. HERSLOFF: Pollajuolo.

Westport House (County Mayo, Ireland). MARQUESS OF SLIGO (EX): Castagno.

Wiesbaden. STÄDTISCHES MUSEUM: Bachiacca, Franciabigio, Granacci, Sellajo.

Williamstown (Mass.). STERLING AND FRANCINE CLARK ART INSTITUTE: Domenico di Michelino, Ridolfo Ghirlandajo.

WILLIAMS COLLEGE: Taddeo Gaddi, Giovanni da Milano.

Windsor Castle. ROYAL COLLECTION: Andrea del Sarto.

Winter Park (Florida). ROLLINS COLLEGE: Rosselli.

Worcester (Mass.). ART MUSEUM: Alunno di Benozzo, Andrea da Firenze, Bronzino, Fra Diamante, Domenico di Michelino, Ridolfo Ghirlandajo, Lorenzo di Credi, Neri di Bicci, Pesellino, Piero di Cosimo, Raffaellino del Garbo, Unidentified Florentine 1350–1420, Unidentified Florentine 1420–1465, Unidentified Florentine 1465–1540.

Wroclaw see Breslau.

Würzburg. MARTIN VON WAGNER MUSEUM: Master of the Bambino Vispo.

York. CITY ART GALLERY: Bachiacca, Bartolomeo di Giovanni, 'Tommaso', 'Utili', Unidentified Florentine 1350–1420.

Zagreb. ART GALLERY: Albertinelli, Fra Angelico, Daddi, Ridolfo Ghirlandajo, Filippino Lippi, Mainardi, Master of S. Miniato, Pesellino, Pier Francesco Fiorentino, Pseudo Pier Francesco Fiorentino, Raffaellino del Garbo, Rosselli, Rossello di Jacopo, Sellajo, Utili.

Zurich. KUNSTHAUS: Daddi, Lorenzo di Niccolò, Masaccio, Pseudo Pier Francesco Fiorentino, Unidentified Florentine 1420–1465.

ANNIE ABEGG-STOCKAR: Botticelli, Domenico Ghirlandajo.

ALFRED E. STEHLI-KAUFMANN: Giovanni dal Ponte.

Homeless. Albertinelli, Alunno di Benozzo, Amedeo da Pistoia, Antonio Veneziano, Bachiacca, Bicci di Lorenzo, Botticini, Bronzino, Cristiani, Domenico di Michelino, Francesco di Antonio, Giotto Assistant, Giotto Follower, Giovanni dal Ponte, Jacopo del Casentino, Machiavelli, Mainardi, Mariotto di Nardo, Maso di Banco, Master of the Bambino Vispo, Master of the Castello Nativity, Master of the Lathrop Tondo, Master of S. Miniato, Michelangelo, Michelangelo Follower, Neri di Bicci, Niccolò di Pietro Gerini, Niccolò di Tommaso, Pier Francesco Fiorentino, Pseudo Pier Francesco Fiorentino, Pontormo, Puligo, Raffaellino del Garbo, Rosselli, Rossello di Jacopo, Sellajo, 'Tommaso', Tommaso di Stefano Lunetti, 'Utili', Unidentified Florentine 1350–1420, Unidentified Florentine 1420–1465.

MADE IN GREAT BRITAIN 1963

PRINTED BY GEO. GIBBONS LTD · LEICESTER

BOUND AT THE PITMAN PRESS · BATH